Receiving the Spirit at Old First Church

Receiving the Spirit
At Old First Church

Arthur A. Rouner Jr.

To Anne + Brad Herman
Dear friends in the Spirit.
With great affection and
admiration, and so many
thanks.
  Arthur Rouner

WIPF & STOCK · Eugene, Oregon

Wipf and Stock Publishers
199 W 8th Ave, Suite 3
Eugene, OR 97401

Receiving the Spirit at Old First Church
By Rouner, Arthur A., Jr.
Copyright©1982 by Rouner, Arthur A., Jr.
ISBN 13: 978-1-5326-0948-0
Publication date 9/30/2016
Previously published by The Pilgrim Press, 1982

Contents

Preface

THIS book comes from a Congregational parish minister who, less than a decade ago, was given the experience of being "baptized with the Holy Spirit" on the front lawn of a Catholic university through the prayer and counsel of a Lutheran minister and author.

It was a freeing and healing personal experience. It was also an experience and a "way" that seemed important for me as a minister to offer kindly but consistently, personally but persistently, to my flock over a period of years for their personal renewal and for the church's power. It has been a long struggle and is by no means done. Yet wonderful blessings have come for the church and for me and my family.

I did write articles for two denominational journals about my own experience, and a literary agent once had what seemed a misguided instinct that I should write a book on the Holy Spirit.

At that time paperback Holy Spirit books, most of them helpful and well-written by people far more deeply involved in the movement and its ministry, were coming on the market by the score. A book on the Spirit seemed somehow not the book I was meant to write at that time.

But a new stage of the development of the charismatic or Holy Spirit movement has recently emerged. This is the advent of the charismatics and the Holy Spirit movement, not only in the Catholic Church followed powerfully by the Lutheran tradition, but now persistently and inevitably among Protestant traditions of free-church order, and some of them of "liberal" theology with deep moral-ministry concerns, and many of them "mainline" in their traditional, leading-citizen community stance.

Many people have greeted this rise with dismay and apprehension. They have also very quickly and, I think, mistakenly dismissed it as theologically "fundamentalist," which to them meant biblicist, rigid, intolerant, emotional, and just not the sort of movement or people who are "our kind." This error in judgment has kept many fair-minded, faithful Christian people in a posture of instinctive resistance to something that God may well be wanting them to welcome and incorporate into their own lives and ministries.

If I can help in some measure to break down those "middle walls" of suspicion and apprehension and to encourage the whole Christian community of the American church, especially those who are most unlikely by their tradition to be open, to give the movement a chance, I will be grateful indeed.

My own people of The Colonial Church of Edina, in Minneapolis, Minnesota, by their questions, protests, discussion, and finally positive and personal response, have helped to fashion what has been written on these pages. Indeed, they are at some points the subject of these pages. They gave me time to be away from the pressures of the parish to write, and for that opportunity and support I am grateful. My own children's willingness to enter into the experience of the Spirit has been a great encouragement to me. My wife's constant challenge to incorporate these deep things of the Spirit into my personal life and the church's life has spurred me on, and my secretary Lois Collings' wonderful willingness, yet again, to type one more manuscript for publication have all made the book possible. I thank them.

Arthur Rouner

Receiving the Spirit at Old First Church

Chapter 1

Signposts and Impressions of the Coming of the Spirit

ONE of the first indicators to me of something brewing in the world of the church, and especially in my own Congregational tradition, was my experience at the International Congregational Council meeting at St. Andrew's in Scotland. As a Union Seminary middler taking that one year at New College, Edinburgh, I was allowed to be a delegate from the United States to that Congregational meeting. It was profoundly influential on my whole understanding of the Congregational way of church life itself, but more importantly on my sense of who the Holy Spirit is and how, in practical pragmatic ways, the Spirit intends to be not only a part, but ruler—divine authority—and leader over each company of Christians gathered together as God's people.

As the council got down to business, the moderator from America pulled out a pocket watch, laid it on the podium, and rather grandly announced that each person in the discussion would be given exactly two minutes to speak, no more, no less.

It was at that moment that the meeting died. Something had gone wrong. The delegates refused to speak at all.

Finally, the vice-moderator, the principal of the Congregational theological college in Edinburgh, gently whispered something to the moderator, and was allowed to take over the meeting. He did away with watches, announced that people could speak as the Spirit led them.

What had happened was that, in the eyes of the British Congregationalists, a fundamental principle had been violated, a basic theological truth had been ignored. The Holy Spirit had been shouldered out of the meeting. And as I later learned from them privately, the whole British delegation was incensed and simply sat on their hands, refusing to budge. Because the Holy Spirit, they said, was essential to the working of the Congregational Church meeting. Indeed, it was the Holy Spirit, they insisted, who was the basic assumption and power, and raison d'etre of the peculiarly Congregational view of the church's authority and function.

Jesus Christ rules his own church through the direct leading and guiding of his Holy Spirit. A high view of the Holy Spirit, I discovered, was a practical and spiritual essential of the Congregational understanding of what a church was. For me this was a whole new vision of the essential reality and necessity of the Holy Spirit in the life of the church. And yet American Congregationalists had lost sight of that essence of their "way."

This insight was to become a touchstone for my own understanding of the church, and for my first struggle to articulate that new/old essential ingredient for church life in a book I called *The Congregational Way of Life*.

Discovery of South American Pentecostalism

It was doubly interesting, then, when I returned the next year for my final theological year at Union Seminary, New York, to have its president, Henry Pitney Van Dusen, confide to me in a private conversation his contention that "the Holy Spirit is the most neglected doctrine in theological study today." That was in 1953.

His statement was especially interesting because, as an ecumenical statesman of unquestioned stature, he was also a leading spokesman for liberal theology in a seminary then dominated by the leaders of neoorthodoxy.

Even more fascinating was learning from an article by Van Dusen in *The Christian Century* that later in the 1950s he discovered the Pentecostals in South America. It was evident to him that their spiritual vitality and living sense of New Testament Christianity was so powerful that it was sweeping South America, bringing to vital life in faith thousands who had never been touched by the, at that time, status-quo-supporting Catholic Church. He ventured to prophesy that Pentecostalism would become the "third great force" in world Christianity.

And yet for saying that, for making that prophecy—which is already being fulfilled—he was essentially laughed out of court, in spite of his credentials as an observer of and leader in world Christianity. The opinion was that something had gone wrong with Pitney, and not that this man who cared so much about God's work in the world had, in fact, put a finger on one of the most significant emerging realities in the church's life in many centuries.

Pentecostalism *was* sweeping South America, and people with no faith or only a traditional faith were coming into new life under the Spirit.

The God Question

Christian theology was struggling with the questions: Who was God? How did God affect and communicate with the world?

The leader of this struggle was Karl Barth in his radical rethinking of the liberal presuppositions that humankind was perfectible, that all one needed was to be more universally and better educated, that the world was getting better and better, and that human beings could and indeed were bringing the kingdom of God on earth.

The Congregationalists in America had incorporated this view into their Kansas City statement of faith adopted at the very end of the 1920s, when it seemed that society could be changed by human genius and skill and faithfulness into a just community that would be the kingdom:

> Depending, as did our fathers, upon the continued guidance of the Holy Spirit to lead us into all truth, we work and pray for the transformation of the world into the kingdom of God, and we look with faith for the triumph of righteousness, and the life everlasting.

Karl Barth, reflecting in the 1920s on a world consumed suddenly in a terrible war and with an agonizing economic depression on its way, saw through the naive simplicities of this glib theology of human and societal perfectibility. He wrote of the God who is completely other than this world and, far from immanent within it, stands outside and hurls the Word at human beings like a rock thrown at their heads.

Barth wrote of the "Word of God" as distinct from the "word of man." It was a high concept of what God's Word in the Bible is to us. Barth's impact was very like the prophet's proclamation. It shook the then comfortable theological world with its thoroughly biblical idea that people do only evil and can do nothing to bring the kingdom.

[4]

And of course Reinhold Niebuhr was influenced both by Barth and by his own experience, in industrialized Detroit where he began as a parish pastor, of society's selfish uncaring for less powerful people. Niebuhr substantiated in his ethical writings Barth's cynicism about human ability to bring in the kingdom. He saw the evil of selfishness as perpetrated particularly through industrialism.

As another world war loomed on Europe's horizon, a young student of Niebuhr's, Dietrich Bonhoeffer, left his graduate studies and teaching at Union Seminary on one of the last ships to leave New York City, to return to his native Germany to stand with his people in the "Confessing church."

Imprisoned for his part in a plot to assassinate Adolph Hitler, Bonhoeffer wrote movingly of the meaning of the Christians' beloved community in his *Life Together.* Then in his *Letters and Papers from Prison* he described how a "religionless Christianity" that is above formal church and the life of the Christian community can sustain the Christian even when he or she is cut off from brothers and sisters and forced to live within a completely secular culture, such as the one he found in prison.

In the late 1950s and early 1960s Bishop John A.T. Robinson of the Church of England borrowed ideas—I think unfairly—from Bonhoeffer and others to institute what became the "Honest to God" movement, lauding secularity and life apart from the church. Robinson combined Bonhoeffer's ideas with Rudolf Bultmann's demythologizing of the New Testament to prepare the way, in fact, for the "death of God" theologians, Thomas Altizer and William Hamilton, for whom, in a world now completely secularized, God no longer spoke and was silent.

The Idolizing of Secularism

Robinson, Altizer, and Hamilton encouraged a whole new fascination with secularism in the American church of the early 1960s. This secularism offered the presumed possibility of a life of faith without the church and, in a real sense, without God. Prayer became simply being and thinking and acting.

Theologian Harvey Cox capitalized on the trend with his immensely popular *Secular City*. Combined with Joseph Fletcher's *Situation Ethics* and the emerging of a "new morality," secularism seemed a perfect theological match for a decade that wanted to do away with all restraints, defeat all disciplines, and overthrow all institutions. The American church, its leaders, and all its eager, young (and some not so young) followers wanted nothing more than to escape from the pieties of the past, from the restrictions of tradition, and to do a new thing.

They were committed to a radical critique of religion as it had been. And they longed, almost abjectly, to move in step with the increasingly radical political protest of the sixties that rightly decried the evils of self-serving and insensitive governments, businesses, and universities, and protested against them with marches and sit-ins.

The Protest of the Sixties

The profound protest first against racism and then against war became the place of the real religion of the 1960s, and the proponents of secularism in theology seemed at first to be in tune with that mood. It was a movement of the people. It was in the streets, where the people are. It brought the buses of Birmingham to a halt, it threatened Selma, and it brought a new day to a changing America. It was in the streets that people were singing, "We shall overcome someday!" It would be "black and white together someday."

Difficult questions were being asked by many people, among them Bob Dylan with his song, "Blowin' in the Wind." Things were changing in the America of the 1960s. Something new was emerging. But it was no secularism that Martin Luther King Jr. preached. It was the Christ who laid down his life and dared to be crucified who was the heart and power of the Southern Christian Leadership Conference. But the blacks were in the streets and everyone was welcome to join them, and so the secularists joined "the movement."

End of Ecclesiastical Ecumenism

It was the streets of the 1960s that destroyed the ecumenical movement as, through the thrust to create one great organization of churches by the negotiating and political manipulation of ecclesiastical bureaucrats, the movement became pointless. After all, now Catholic and Protestant, nun and priest, minister and layperson, black and white, Episcopalian and Presbyterian were together. The march on Selma did that. The march on Washington did that. The silent vigils for Vietnam war dead did that. The rise of a new pacifism did that.

The ecumenical movement—at least as the peculiar province of denominational leaders—became too tame for a day in which, somehow, through a deep, life-demanding human and divine cause, its most practical human goals had already been achieved. Now it was too ecclesiastical. Now it was beside the point.

The Holy Spirit, mysteriously and unexpectedly, had

done in the streets what ecclesiastical machinery had been unable to do either at altars or at council tables.

The Protests Turn Sour

But something happened to the protests when first Martin Luther King Jr. and then Robert Kennedy was shot. They were, of course, not the only ones to lose their lives in the cause. But their murders brought to the surface every anger against prejudice and entrenched self-interest that Americans young or old had ever felt, and suddenly those without faith, those who cared little for Brother Martin's Jesus, came to leadership, and Black Panthers and Simbianese Liberation Armies had their day. Cynicism overtook the movement, and despair of ever changing entrenched white capitalist society set in; anger turned to violence, and bombs went off, and banks were robbed, and heiresses were kidnapped, and terrorism arose—indeed, on a world scale.

The unmasking of America's own evil in the invasion of Cambodia and the Watergate break-in, brought, beyond the violence, deep disillusionment, and many wondered "what's the use?"

The Turning Inward

It seemed natural, therefore, for America to turn inward in the early 1970s. The drug movement came and, I believe, behind and beneath it, the search for meaning.

Following the drug culture's vogue, a new discovery was made by young people of the "high" of meditation, and then of the new possibilities of Christianity. Communes became Christian communes. The Jesus movement emerged in southern California, and suddenly post-hippie protesting young people were being baptized in the ocean.

The scene was set for the emergence in America of something beautiful for God, something new, yet very old: the coming of the Holy Spirit.

Preparing the Way

All this, I believe, was part of preparing the way for the coming of the Holy Spirit to the American church.

The Pentecostal movement as a classic form antedated all this fifties, sixties, and seventies history. It became identifiable at the very beginning of the twentieth century in a little congregation at the Azusa Street Chapel in Los Angeles. Signs of the Spirit were evidenced there in a way that had not been recorded in the church's life since the first and second centuries.

That chapel and its congregation birthed Aimee Semple McPherson and the Foursquare Gospel Church. The Assemblies of God and several other churches came into an experience of the Spirit of God that was emotional, and life-changing, and seemed forbidding to most mainline liberal Protestants.

One of the tragedies of the twentieth-century American church is that liberal Protestantism was so stung by the fundamentalist controversy of the 1920s involving Harry Emerson Fosdick and the Presbyterian denomination, that it has since consistently failed to distinguish the strands of theological conviction, biblical position, and human concern of Evangelicalism and Pentecostalism, failing to realize that these movements are not the same as early twentieth-century fundamentalism.

In fact, fundamentalism has had more to do with an attitude of mind and spirit than it has primarily to do with a biblical viewpoint. In narrowness of vision, blindness to other views, rigidity, and judgmental spirit, theological liberalism has often outdone the fundamentalists.

The Rise of Experiential Religion

What classic Pentecostalism meant, and what the protest marches of a very different group of Christians meant, was that a new experiential religion was growing in America. People were feeling God in their hearts, and seeing God at work around them and invading their lives. They were experiencing God. Faith had an authentic ring for them. God, they discovered, was coming within them with the "sighs too deep for utterance" of speaking in tongues, coming in gifts of healing, of organization, of teaching and healing.

Two Mysterious Connections

From the tradition of so-called classic Pentecostalism came a white South African named David DuPlessis. He is considered by many to be the father—or at least the father figure—of the more recent charismatic movement that is touching all denominations and traditions.

I was privileged in 1972 at the sixth annual conference on the Holy Spirit of the Catholic Church at Notre Dame University, to hear that seventy-year-old valiant Christian leader tell a remarkable story of how he, as a classic, oldline Pentecostal (a tradition that was then largely fundamentalist), came into a new connection, a new Christian relationship, and what that had meant, not only for him, but quite probably for the whole Christian church.

He addressed some five hundred of us (a small group meeting at that conference of eleven thousand!) outdoors on a Sunday afternoon. He told of the suspicions he had been brought up with about mainline Protestantism, and certainly about Catholicism. Clearly, the political and social activists of the National Council and World Council of Churches were anathema to the tradition in which he was raised.

One day, while a guest in the home of a fellow Pentecostal minister he had a vision that came as a dream in the night. God called him specifically and unequivocally to go to the leaders of the National and World Councils of Churches, and befriend them, and share his insights about the Holy Spirit with them.

His friend as much as told him he was crazy and that such a move would defy all that his denominational tradition stood for. But he knew it was a call from God, and so he went to those national and world Christian leaders. They did not understand him at first. But he persisted. They became friends. He had opportunity to talk with them about what he felt the Bible was saying about the crucial importance of the Holy Spirit to the church. They began to listen.

More importantly, a priest attached to the Roman Curia in those earliest days of Pope John's brief pontificate became fascinated with the story the aging DuPlessis was telling and the persuasive scriptural argument he presented. The priest asked if he might take that theory and viewpoint to Rome and to the papal offices. Was it a coincidence that it was Pope John who personally opened the windows of the Catholic Church to a new understanding and expectation of the Holy Spirit?

David DuPlessis dared to believe that God had prepared the American and the world church for the message of the Spirit, and that he had been given the opportunity to be its bearer and ambassador. It was a humbling and thrilling story of a man who was obedient to the heavenly vision and dared "to go over into Macedonia" to help.

The fullness of time. The *kairos*. God's ripe moment. And a man who was willing to risk a great deal to be the instrument.

And then in the early 1960s came the first sign on the mainline Protestant side of the outbreaking of the Spirit in a way new and different from turn-of-the-century classical Pentecostalism.

An Episcopal priest named Dennis Bennett, rector of a suburban Los Angeles parish of two thousand members, received the Holy Spirit. He worked underground for a while, sharing his experience with a small few in his church.

When he finally announced publicly that he had received the baptism of the Holy Spirit, there was dismay on the part of one of his associates who stripped off his own robes and dramatically left the chancel condemning Bennett's experience of the Spirit and his attempt finally to bring it to the life of that parish.

As he has later said, he came out in the open too late, and ultimately he felt he had to leave that parish and take his ministry of the Spirit elsewhere—eventually to the whole country.

DuPlessis and Bennett were very different men, but each was a sign and a testimony that God was coming in the Spirit, and the church had better watch out.

In the years since Dennis Bennett's early signaling in 1962 of the coming of the Spirit to the mainline churches of American Protestantism, and Pope John's opening of the windows of the Catholic Church of the world to the Spirit's power, a dramatic growth has come in the Spirit-experience for all kinds of Christians, and all kinds of churches.

Gifted teachers in the ways of the Spirit have been called out and sent on their way, crisscrossing the country to reassure fearful Christians about the Spirit and opening up new avenues for God's work and healing: Dennis Bennett and Terry Fullam for the Episcopalians, and also Graham Pulkingham with his people's experimenting and pioneering in Houston's Church of the Redeemer in the meaning of community; the prayer fellowships at the Catholic Duquesne and Notre Dame universities, with their profound influence in gathering the annually growing Catholic conference on the Holy Spirit; and Father Francis McNutt, who emerged as one of American Catholicism's most articulate advocates for the Spirit movement and as its most gifted teacher and practitioner of Christian healing.

Large and significant communities of the Spirit have grown up in Ann Arbor, Michigan and in Minneapolis, Minnesota. Annual conferences on the Holy Spirit have now been held for nearly a decade by the Lutheran Church, with special leadership coming from the North Heights Lutheran Church in the northern suburbs in Minneapolis. The Presbyterians, the American Baptists, and now even the United Church of Christ, with its Congregational Christian and Evangelical and Reformed background, are also among those denominations holding annual conferences on the Holy Spirit.

Within little more than a decade a new literature has developed. Scores of excellent paperback books have been produced by the Holy Spirit movement, pointing the way and documenting the experience of the Holy Spirit among the people of God today.

Henry Van Dusen might have been surprised. I hope he would have been glad. He spoke as a prophet on the seminary steps more than twenty-five years ago, and he had a significant part, courageous and costly, in perceiving and promoting what God had decided it was time to do in the church in America and in the world.

[13]

Chapter 2

Why Did It Take Me So Long to Receive the Spirit?

ONLY God sends the Spirit, and does it when ready to do so. Evidently, the Spirit is sent when the world is ready and the time is right.

The Spirit's coming may require a time when everything else is so bad that only then will people seriously entertain the thought of the Spirit. It may require a readiness on the part of the church or the world to welcome the Spirit in a way in which they were previously unwilling to do.

But mostly the Spirit's coming is a surprise—as Jesus explained very carefully to Nicodemus the churchman. And the Spirit has come as a very great and wonderful surprise to the church of the third quarter of the twentieth century.

What God's design might be is, to most of us, not clear yet. But what God has done, and who has been used in sending the Spirit in the church since the early 1960s is clear enough for those who will look back and recollect.

What I write here for my brother and sister ministers—and for lay leaders of parish churches—are my own reflections. I have obviously not written history here, but rather have recollected a series of signposts. They form a kind of collage that at least reminds me of where the church has been and how wonderfully far it has come in the way of the Spirit during the twenty-five years I have been an ordained minister.

My Personal Search for the Holy Spirit

In telling anything to my brother and sister Christians in the church and in the professional ministry about the work of the Holy Spirit in our day as I have seen the Spirit in the life of the parish church I serve, it is important to be quite personal. In this chapter I want to tell something of my own pilgrimage of faith and how the Holy Spirit has come to loom large in my life.

On Being a Spirit Person

As I look back over my life I have the sense that I was always what I would call a "Spirit person." That means that the "things of the Spirit" interested me. I cared about Christian experience in prayer and devotion from an early age. I have probably always been more a heart person than a head person. The more emotional, Baptist side of my religious background came through my mother, the daughter of a Baptist minister and a woman Baptist missionary, and has always seemed a more congenial and natural stream in my own spirit than the much more rational philosophical inheritance I received from my Congregational minister father.

The "things of God" were never a problem for me. I had no agonizing struggle to believe in God. The miracles of Jesus and the power of the Spirit manifested in the life of the first-century church always seemed utterly logical to me.

I grew up believing in prayer and in the power and reality of intercession for others. As a young minister in a country parish I prayed for my people, gathered a little prayer group among them, rejoiced with them in the wonder of prayers answered with miracles in our midst, and I was open to learning whatever there was to be learned about prayer.

In my hospital calling I always either laid a hand on or simply held the hand of the person I was visiting, and prayed. When a brother minister suggested I'd be a natural to attend an Agnes Sanford "School of Pastoral Care" on Christian healing at Whitinsville, Massachusetts, it was very easy to say "I'll go there." Agnes Sanford confirmed me in what I already felt about healing. And of course she taught me a great deal I had not known and encouraged me all the more to continue and expand the healing ministry as part of my own, wherever I could serve. I've tried to do that.

I knew that it is the Spirit who brings the triune God to us, and that none of us as Christians today would even know of Jesus and "the Father" without the continual working of the Spirit in our world and in our lives.

My Own Stages of Growth

My first remembered turning point of faith came when Gil Dodds, the great indoor miler of the 1940s, came to our town of Portsmouth, New Hampshire as an evangelist. There I was, at the last "crusade" meeting in the auditorium of the junior high school, with my minister father on the platform as a leading minister of the community, blessing the occasion somewhat unwillingly, and Gil Dodds preaching and finally issuing a call to all those who wanted to commit themselves to Christ to come forward.

I went—with my eleven-year-old brother (I was twelve) struggling to hold me back. But I knew I had to go, whatever the public display might be. Carl Unger, the trombonist, led me into the kingdom. I wept and was glad I had done it.

While that public commitment by the number one son, who presumably should have already come to Christ in his own home, was hard on my father, my mother understood and helped me make it an honest beginning.

Later, when I was a first-year theological student at Union Seminary, the darkness rolled in through the drowning of a twelve-year-old boy of my seventh grade Sunday school class during a Saturday afternoon swim in the pool of the Madison Avenue Presbyterian Church in New York. The very spirit of the seminary seemed to add to the gloom.

A Scottish preacher named James Stewart came to New York in Holy Week of that year and preached in the Union Seminary chapel on Good Friday on "The Rending of The Veil." It was the very opening of the doors of heaven to me, and I decided then and there that I would go where that man was.

His life as "a man in Christ" became a second turning point for me as my wife and I went to Scotland so that I could take my middler year there with Stewart, Principal John Baillie, Tom Torrance, and others on that great faculty. It was the witness of James Stewart's life and ministry that rescued and healed my own spirit and helped me to see what it could mean, at least for me, to be a minister.

A decade later a retreat with Campus Crusade for Christ staff members near the Twin Cities in Minnesota again became an important firing of my spirit and deepening of my faith.

All along the way I was learning more about the Spirit: a bit of reading here, an insight from conversation there, and always the witness of the book of Acts and Pentecost itself.

I knew from my own studies, from the insights of the English Congregationalists, and from my research into the Savoy Platform of 1658 in London, that the Spirit was the heart of Congregational theology, that the Pilgrims were Holy Spirit people as well as Bible people and Jesus people, trusting in God's guidance for their decisions in Church Meeting.

In fact, a fairly reasonable picture of the Holy Spirit's Person and work was right there in the final chapter of my first book, *The Congregational Way of Life,* written during 1957-58 in my first church and published in 1960.

I look back now and realize that I said it then without personally having had the full experience of the Spirit. It is enough to make me feel that the Spirit of God was working with me, and using me even at a time when I did not fully realize it myself, or at least had not had the breakthrough experience of being baptized or overwhelmed and filled by the Spirit in a personal Pentecost event.

Being Sought by the Spirit

Most of the years from 1962 to 1972—the first ten years of my ministry at The Colonial Church of Edina—were years of more and more intense interest in who the Holy Spirit is.

During a dark personal time in my life at the end of the 1960s when the country was in political and moral turmoil, and Martin Luther King Jr. and Robert Kennedy were assassinated, and my own personal life was not right with God, and I wasn't sure I wouldn't do better to leave the ministry and make a try at politics, or at just going away and trying to write a novel, or just going away—I came to know more and more clearly that I wanted and needed "something more"—the Spirit—in my life.

During those late sixties years I was part of a little ministerial prayer group of variously five to seven clerical brothers in our town who met weekly in the late afternoon for an hour or two mostly to laugh and talk about our ministries and our burdens and struggles, and to pray for one another. It became a deeply intimate fellowship of support and understanding that eventually came literally to save my life from the darkness.

One afternoon in the early winter of 1967, several of these men laid hands in prayer upon me and prayed for the coming of the Holy Spirit upon me with tongues and with fire. I knelt to receive their prayers. My back, aching from a ruptured disk, had me in physical pain. My heart, I felt, was not right with anyone—God, my wife, my church, my kids, myself. I was miserable and, as I later came to realize, a very poor candidate for baptism with the Holy Spirit.

By that night the back pain was so excruciating that I found myself on my hands and knees on the floor of a local restaurant where I had gone with my family to celebrate the twelfth birthday of our oldest son. I was carted off home, visited by our family doctor, and taken to the hospital that night. By the following week I was undergoing disk surgery and spending a fair part of the lenten season attempting to recuperate physically and finding my way again spiritually. I continued to pursue and explore the Spirit—rather, the Spirit was pursuing and exploring me.

The Catholic "Community of Light," a growing charismatic community in Minneapolis, came to be of great interest to me, and we brought several of their leaders to address small groups of Colonial Church people about their experience of the Holy Spirit. I began to read more and more about the Spirit and about others' experience of the Spirit.

A change began to take place in Colonial Church as a change took place in me. As my body healed, my heart and soul began to heal. Having been through the valley, I found I could understand more compassionately others who were going through the valley. I became strangely freer to love people. Love began to grow as a mark of the life of the Colonial Church. A transformation was at work in the midst of us.

Finally, in 1972, after ten years as the church's senior minister, I was granted the wonderful privilege of a twelve-week sabbatical time of study and exploration away from the church.

My great curiosity was to see what was happening to the rest of the church in America, and particularly to see if the love we were experiencing in Colonial was happening in other churches and Christian communities. I decided that I would travel about incognito and visit Christian communities in America and in Europe and try to see where the Spirit was at work in them, and particularly whether the coming of the Spirit turned them in upon themselves, as a kind of hoarding of their light and experience, or if it turned them outward to the world in loving service to others.

Finding and Being Found

At my first stop I found, or was found by, the Spirit. At least, the search ended, and a new beginning was made. It is dated in my heart by the year and the place. 1972. In the spring. On a university campus. Among the Benedictines. In Minnesota.

I went in mid-May as a Bush Foundation fellow for two weeks of personal study at the Benedictine seminary connected with the Abbey and University of St. John's in Collegeville, Minnesota. It was intended as a study opportunity for middle-aged Protestant clerics to go apart to a seminary setting, have a little monk's cell of their own, read and pray, pursue any project they might like, use the university's library, worship both with the monks in the abbey and daily with the theological students of the seminary, enjoy the fellowship of other students, and perhaps do some solid work.

The Benedictine professors made it clear that the four Protestant ministers in their midst were welcome to worship with the seminary community each afternoon at five o'clock, and to share in receiving the Eucharist. Those became times of joy and high privilege.

Over lunch I revealed my personal search and my interest in the Holy Spirit and in community. That's all some of those young seminarians needed to hear. "If you're interested in the Holy Spirit and in community," they said, "you're in the right place. Come with us to our Caedman Prayer Group at the college of St. Benedict this Wednesday. The other thing you should do is meet the three men studying as scholars at the Ecumenical Institute and read the books each of them has written on the Holy Spirit."

I did both. The "prayer group" was a company of at least one hundred who gathered in a college lecture hall to sing beautiful Spirit songs, to hear scripture read, a homily given, personal testimony shared, and generally to be lifted high in an uncommon charismatic experience of joy in Jesus. People of all ages and, I am sure, stages, were there. Cute, free-spirited, miniskirted, beaded nuns without habits, graying oldsters from the town, eager students of both sexes from two colleges and the seminary, a few scattered priests—and me.

Clearly, the Spirit of God was there. I was overjoyed. I was getting close.

In the meantime, I was kneeling by my bed at night trying on my own to make the funny sounds of speaking in tongues—but to no avail. By day I was reading the three excellent books on the Spirit written by Protestant charismatic movement leaders who were present on six-month study periods at St. John's Ecumenical Institute: Arnold Bittlinger of the Lay Academy movement of Germany; J. Rodman Williams of the Presbyterian theological faculty in Austin, Texas; and Larry Christenson, a Lutheran pastor from southern California.

On the last day of my two weeks there I finally snagged all three for lunch. "Tell me about the Spirit, and the baptism," I asked. "I've been trying, and still don't seem a very good candidate," I confessed. "I remember that when Agnes Sanford, the healer, prayed for me she prophesied a pastoral setting for my healing ministry. Clearly, I wasn't to be an Oral Roberts or a Kathryn Kuhlmann. Maybe with my big suburban parish I'm just supposed to be open and encouraging and lead others to the Spirit, but not supposed to be baptized with the Spirit myself or have the gift of tongues for my own . . ."

They chuckled tolerantly and allowed that in their understanding any and every Christian may and can receive the baptism and have the gift of tongues—and, of course, other gifts as well.

The luncheon broke up, and Larry Christenson said,

"Come out on the lawn, Arthur, and let's talk and pray about this a little farther."

When we were settled, looking up at the beauty of the great abbey church above us, Larry Christenson said, "It didn't work, just saying a lot of sounds, did it? Only the Spirit can make the break through that barrier and bring out your own unknown language of praise, which God has given you. It's really already there, down inside. Sometimes the words have already formed themselves and you've said them unspokenly to yourself—haven't you?" I acknowledged that yes, in fact, I thought I had! I confessed, as so many others have, that I hadn't realized that's what it was. "After all," Larry said, "the Bible says the Spirit groans within us, with sighs too deep for utterance."

Then he prayed for me, that I would indeed be baptized by the mighty Spirit of God, and find my whole ministry touched by that Spirit, and that I would be given, among other gifts, the particular gift of speaking in tongues, so that I would know that the Spirit of God had touched me, and was in me, and had filled me with power for ministry, and that I would be free to have joy in my faith and service.

I mumbled in response a few syllables which seemed strange and stumbling and totally inadequate to me. But Larry did not say anything like: "You jerk, that's not right, what a poor student you are!" He was an encouragement. "That's right. That's a start. All you have to do now is practice your new language, go in peace, and be glad." We said something like "Praise the Lord!" together, hugged each other, and parted.

It was, it seemed to me, an inept beginning. But it was a beginning.

I have realized, on reflection, that I felt an increasing

embarrassment, the closer I got to Larry's prayer and to the actual moment of my making that audible, unknown, uncontrolled sound. I have come to realize that that was peculiarly the preacher's embarrassment and fear. I was a man who believed in the power of the Word of God, who loved words and knew their importance, who therefore was committed by faith and by profession to saying what he meant to say, and who felt a need to have some control over those words. And I was, therefore, not only "uptight" but monumentally embarrassed to be about to let that preacherly tongue go (along with whatever dignity or grace it may have had) and be used to say words and make sounds I couldn't even understand—indeed, sounds that would appear foolish to me and to anyone who might hear them.

Even now, when it occasionally seems right to pray in tongues in church on Pentecost, or in a healing prayer for someone in the midst of our little weekly "pulpit communion" after church on Sunday, or privately in my study for someone who has come in need, or at a hospital bedside where I am not sure just what is the right prayer to pray in English, the sound seems strange at first and I'm almost embarrassed to go on. Yet always it seems to minister peace, and healing, and joy, and power to others, and to me, and I sense again how much it was a prayer the Holy Spirit was giving me to pray.

The words seem almost to be a language of their own. "Savarente—to dio-molo-codiante. Shadamante calliente . . ." And so on it goes. To me, beautiful words that flow with an almost Latin or Spanish sound, bringing a lilt to my voice and a lift to my spirit.

For the next weeks of the summer I did practice "my language"—driving down the interstate toward Chicago and Cincinnati, up to Notre Dame, out across South

Dakota, and especially out the car window at 80 mph (in those pre-gas-shortage days!) across the prairies and meadows of Montana as the search and research continued.

Discovering the Spirit Places

The sabbatical time was important not just for my own faith. It was important for its new view of the Spirit's communities, and the insights it offered into how such communities are gathered, and the many forms they take, and a little bit of what their significance is. As far as how the Spirit came to me and into the life of Colonial Church, the sabbatical search at least delineates the influences God was using in affecting how we as a church were to measure our life and to grow.

Where to go resulted from the interested comments and letters and bits of advice of friends who said, "Oh, visiting Christian communities, eh? Have you heard of the thus-and-such center, or of so-and-so who is significant for this or that?" The Spirit brought the experience of many people together in simply determining my itinerary as well as my teachers and my new friends in faith that summer.

In early June I packed my Mustang with rucksack, sleeping bag, books, camera, legal pads, and pens, put on my jeans and boots, and headed south toward Chicago.

The summer took me to old friends in ministry and mission whose work I had never seen, it took me to a Christian commune, and to a couple of traditional churches where interesting things of the Spirit were happening. It took me to an Amish bishop's home in Indiana, to the annual national gathering of the Catholic charismatic movement. It took me to three different denominational retreat houses or centers of renewal. It took me to the living rooms or dinner tables of three or four fellow ministers—one a leader in the mainline charismatic movement, and another a friendly skeptic about "all of this Jesus emphasis." It took me to several rather creative, seminal churches in California, and it took me to three or four vital and very different centers of Christian renewal in Europe.

There were names like the Lutheran's Holden Village in Chelan, Washington; the Presbyterian's Ghost Ranch in the Southwest; Garden Grove Community Church, Hollywood and Bel Aire Presbyterian Churches and Peninsula Bible Church in Palo Alto—all in California. In Europe there were names like the Sisters of Mary in Darmstadt, Germany; the Brothers of Taize and the Benedictines of Solemnes, both in France; and Francis and Edith Schaeffer's famous L'Abri community in Switzerland.

They were all very different. They had quite different things to teach me about life in the Spirit for any group of Christians trying to live together. I'm not at all sure I've directly applied anything of what I learned from them to the Colonial Church situation. But those learnings did become part of me and, I suspect, changed me in some ways that have affected my own church's life and what I have since tried to do here.

Learnings from the Summer Sabbatical

My two weeks as a student in the Catholic seminary of St. John's University introduced me to the radical freedom of the Benedictines who, for instance, were able to get away with inviting us Protestants to share fully with them in their daily chapel celebration of the Eucharist.

Their genuine "passing of the peace" in a warm embrace encouraged me to know that that expression of Christian affection was historic and universal, and that I was on the right track in insisting on its place in the wor-

ship service of Colonial Church. Their courage to build
bridges and be ecumenical in the deepest spiritual sense
also encouraged me. Their use of folk songs in worship encouraged me to pursue this at home.

And, of course, my first experience within the free-
moving Catholic form of charismatic worship came in a
university prayer group at St. John's. Their way of leading
the laypeople, especially in music, showed me something
of how this could be done, and has been a model for me in
trying to develop the same kind of easy Spirit worship as
part of a Sunday evening worship at Colonial Church.

Seeing on the signboard of his church in Cincinnati that
my minister friend there was preaching a sermon on the
Holy Spirit, and hearing personally of his own struggling
to understand the Holy Spirit theologically, and his daring
to experiment in his own church and family with "living
in community," became one of the powerful illustrations
to me that the Holy Spirit as Person really is moving across
the face of this land and causing church leaders in many
unlikely places to come to terms with what this means. It
also helped me see doctrinally that who the Holy Spirit is,
and how the Spirit fits with the church's understanding of
God and of God's action and power in the world, is one of
the most critical issues in theology today.

Seeing the home of the Amish bishop in New Berne, Indiana, and the Reba Place fellowship in Evanston, and the
Brothers of Taize, and the Sisters of Mary in Darmstadt,
and even the very medieval life of the brothers in the
Benedictine abbey of Solemnes, made it dramatically clear
to me that many Christians today are experimenting in ut-
ter seriousness with the claims of Christ's call to Christian
community, and that this community is not only possible
but is working in many places where Christians have been
serious about it. I became convinced that ordinary Chris-

tians can find ways, even in modern America, to live out some form of the ideal of community in Christ.

It was especially interesting to me to hear how important the economic factor had been for the Reba Place fellowship. This group had come out of a broadly Mennonite background, so the simple life was already something of an ideal for them. But "it was when we eschewed individual property," the members said, that the knot of competition was cut for them and they were able truly to give themselves in love to one another and to the world.

They, incidentally, were one of the communities whose discovery of a deep life in the Spirit together had opened them up to an even deeper social involvement in the world around them. Reba Place had been so committed to serving a nearby children's hospital in Evanston as volunteers that, in order to be more skilled in their volunteer service, they commissioned and paid for two people of their fellowship to study for master's degrees in psychology so that they could train and sensitize the rest of the community to be more effective and professional in their volunteering! (A very interesting model for the local church!)

Seeing eleven thousand Catholics and Protestants together in a peculiarly moving combination of free Spirit expression in public worship yet held in some order by the enclosing forms of the Catholic mass demonstrated again to me how truly a certain dignity and order and beauty can be combined with and set a context for a very great and winsome freedom and joy.

I loved the experience of all those people singing in the Spirit together as the whole company was caught up in singing chords together in the voices of their many "tongues." ("O, for a thousand tongues to sing/ My great

Redeemer's praise!'') It made me feel "it can be done at Colonial Church.'' Singing in the Spirit, and the full expression of the gifts, especially those expressions of joy and praise and teaching and prophecy and healing, are a viable ideal, even for a mainline, traditional church like mine.

People like Dennis Bennett convinced me that the ideal of the Spirit was worth pursuing, that there were churches like his Episcopal church in Seattle where it was working and where I and my people could find aid and comfort if we needed it as we would begin to be much more explicit about our intentions to open up worship more and more for the Spirit's leading. Even Browne Barr's honest hesitations about this "Spirit thing" and the Jesus movement, along with his own humility as a minister and his great record of deep commitment as a daring, courageous, and moral minister who had challenged so much of establishment thinking within the leadership of the United Church of Christ and Congregational churches, became a sign to me that even in the honest challenge to thoughtful ministers who weren't yet buying it theologically, the Holy Spirit clearly was alive and making an impact upon us all, causing us to dare to think about this strange possibility for the church.

In southern California I saw "Melody Land" Christian Center in Anaheim and Calvary Chapel in Costa Mesa at worship on a Sunday evening each with at least two thousand people gathered for singing, praying, and teaching-preaching time. It was a wonder! Brother Andrew of Corrie Ten Boom fame was holding forth endlessly to the Anaheim company, and the Rev. Chuck Smith in Costa Mesa preached his way through three of the pastoral books of the New Testament in one evening! I felt strangely like Eutychus of falling-asleep-in-church fame. But the witness there was the power of the scriptures and of a very simple commentary about them to be absolutely compelling to hundreds of utterly serious blue-jeaned and now Bible-toting young people.

There was no band, no organ, no tricks, no high jinks, no onstage support to make it all "fun" at Calvary Chapel. Chuck Smith just started singing all by himself, and people followed. He was "it" for hours. There was no overwrought emotionalism with fundamentalist overtones. There was nothing "hyped up" about the experience, except the obvious eagerness of many people to learn from the Bible and to come to know the Spirit. Very sobering and instructive for this particular parish minister! I have not tried to emulate that experience. But I have become convinced that the people will go a long way for something in faith that is real, to see and hear a minister-leader who is authentic, and to be among other people who are honestly looking for something.

This was very supportive of my own conviction that the model of the pilgrim as a stance of growth, and seeking, and following the Holy Spirit together with others into an unknown future—like Abraham of old, and then Moses and his people, and America's own Pilgrims of Plymouth—is compelling and hopeful to the increasing number of unchurched but believing and now actively searching people who are out there in our American cities and towns today. What tremendous potential for the churches—particularly if we ministers can take that longing as seriously as Chuck Smith did.

Observing ministers forget that Chuck Smith was, until barely ten years ago, a faithful, regular, maybe plodding minister like the rest of us, when quite suddenly the Holy Spirit captured his life and energized him with a new vision and therefore a new ministry. It was he who began baptizing young people in the Pacific Ocean.

At Colonial we had for several years already been conducting an annual "lake baptism" at a crowded beach in the City of Minneapolis. The Costa Mesa experience was at the very least an encouragement that we were on the right track.

Just an evening with Bill and Ruth Starr of the Young Life organization in Colorado Springs became a confirmation of a fresh wind of change and openness to the mainline churches, and of support from that youthful arm of the world church in our day.

The seriousness of Francis Schaeffer's L'Abri witness in a critique of modern Western culture, while heavy with a tendency in that community to take itself almost too seriously, nevertheless offered a view of the power of the Christian community to stand over against the prevailing culture and its destructive assumptions, and to confront it and change it. I needed to know that there were others really doing that—that I wasn't alone in it, fighting the destructive forces at work in my suburban town—and that the Spirit was *the source* of power for that fight.

And so the summer went, and so the experiences and the impact of these one or two dozen companies of Christians round the world intensified for me and left their own deep impression on my life. None of them seemed to say I was off the track in my ministry and in my newly-deepened concern for the Holy Spirit and for the reality of Christian community. On the contrary, they confirmed that the Spirit of love that had been growing in Colonial Church was not a fluke, but that it represented our peculiar experience of the Holy Spirit, and gave an assurance that we as a congregation, and I as a minister, were living in a time of high potential for the church, if we were brave enough to dare to move with the Spirit, not hang back in fear, but take the tide at the full, and go for it—even though many in my church might not under-stand, and might even leave.

What I saw out there across the country said, "This ex-perience of the Spirit you've had, Arthur, is right, it is of God, who wants it for you, it's for a purpose, there is a lot ahead—good and bad—that you cannot even imagine now, but the risk it demands of you can be taken bravely, and God will not fail you, as God has not failed these others. So hang on—and go for it!"

I have "gone for it," and the story of what happened to me, and to Colonial Church and its mission, may be worth telling as a vital part of the larger story of how I believe God's Spirit is bidding to break through into all the "Old First Churches" of America—and the world.

Chapter 3

The Spirit and the New Community

MY own search for the Spirit had grown out of my experience of "community" as a profound and growing love within the life of The Colonial Church of Edina. There was an intangible and fragile gift that had come to be the acknowledged mark of the life and worship of that unique congregation of people. I loved them very much. They loved one another. And they had found a way to love the strangers who wandered into their worship and life in increasing numbers.

The growth of that spirit was recognized by many as a change in that church's life, and a dramatic one even though it took place over several years.

That spirit of love had been there healing and working in me. I knew it was real. And I knew enough other churches to know it was not as common to the church as it was intended to be, that it was both rare and wonderful, and that even if I had been in some way an instrument for bringing it, it was not something to be taken for granted or treated in any way lightly or cavalierly by me.

Upon my return from my sabbatical of the Spirit in 1972, the question for me as minister to this unusual company was how to move ahead to claim all the gifts of the Spirit and to do what the New Testament experience appeared to call for in creating that even newer and more wonderful community of love in the Spirit, which seemed surely to be ahead for us—but at the same time to go through that uncertain process without jeopardizing the life of love that was already there.

It was a new thing. I had been with perfectly ordinary-looking people who, when gathered together, had begun to hum and sing in what had swelled into a music for all the world like an angel chorus, and then had died away. When singing together, and praying, most of them raised their arms with hands outstretched, palms raised, and eyes closed. At first, there in the ice arena at Notre Dame, it had made me very uncomfortable. But soon I was overwhelmed with the beauty of it.

On the last day of that Catholic charismatic conference, while a singing group played and all the eleven thousand people began to gather on the greensward outside the Notre Dame library preparing for the last procession to the arena for the final, climactic service, I had watched a young girl of perhaps sixteen or seventeen wearing jeans, standing reverently still, facing the great library wall with her arms outstretched and her head tilted upward. It was a beautiful attitude of awestruck prayer. After watching her a few minutes and being touched deeply in my heart by her young, ingenuous faith, I followed her gaze upward toward the huge wall of the great university library. There, in mosaic, was the figure of Jesus which I had only barely noticed. What was startling was the realization that Jesus Christ himself, in that giant mosaic, was standing with his arms and hands raised, in exactly the position of that young girl who clearly loved him so.

And then, too, there were moments of prayer when these people broke out into beautiful sounds of other languages—tongues—both all together in praise from their seats, and in specific "prophecies" spoken into the microphones for the whole assembly to hear.

Had I been able to bring the whole Colonial congregation there to be part of that great experience, or been able to take them along to the Amish bishop's house, or let them sit with my minister friends Jerry Kirk in Cincinnati, or Roger Frederikson in Sioux Falls, or Dennis Bennett in Seattle, or experience Taize, or see L'Abri, or listen to vespers in Solemnes, or just meet those devoted, miracle-believing Sisters of Mary in Darmstadt, it would all have been so easy. They would have said, "Oh yes, Arthur, we see what you mean. This is of God. We want it in our lives, we want it in Colonial Church. By all means, let us grow in the joy and knowledge of the Spirit!"

But, of course, it was not that way. It was only me going back to them with a heart full of joy and a spirit free, but with a mind and pastoral sense whereby I knew that I alone would have to convey all this experience to them. Deep inside I knew it would be hard for some. I didn't know one deacon would leave the board in dismay, or that others, my dear friends and fellow workers—some very close and important to me—would think I had "gone off the deep end," that I had actually cracked emotionally, that I was now leading the church away from human and social concern and into an alien, self-centered, obscurantist emotionalism.

If I had known all the pain ahead I might not have tried. Today, I look back and see how many have come to accept the charismatic elements of worship and life, and know that God's hand was in it, and the Spirit was with us, and it all has been worth every pain and every heartache, and even every lost friendship along the way.

I began by teaching as faithfully as I could, the little I knew. Out of a changing group of one hundred who came to those Wednesday evenings, there were future deacons and leaders of that congregation who came forward on the last night to have hands laid upon them and prayers asked for the coming of the Spirit and the work of the baptism in their lives.

Among them came my own oldest son and daughter. I learned later that for them the first twenty-four hours were confusing and they were not sure what, if anything, had happened. And then it came—the speaking in tongues, the full joy.

I was not the most scared and uncertain. But I was close. Always there were the awful questions: What if it doesn't work? What if nothing happens? What if no lives are touched and there is no evidence of the Spirit's coming, no signs of Pentecostal fire, no tongues, no joy, no second birth?

I had to be crazy to risk the good thing that we had going at Colonial. Particularly, to do it during the very time when the church was agonizing its way through a series of decisions to leave our old and beloved church building and neighborhood, buy a twenty-three-acre site two and one-half miles away, raise the money to build a three-and-one-half-million-dollar "meetinghouse" and "New England Village" complex as our new church.

Not only was the New England architectural emphasis galling to some, but the very decision dismayed others, and when it came to fund-raising many of them were not only not there to help, but also not there to give, and finally not even there to be part of our life.

It was a heartbreaking time. Several people hinted and one church council member wrote to me and the council three times urging me to accept the fact that thirteen years had been too long and that it was time for me to leave.

I took him seriously, and almost did leave. A New York church called me, and, at the request of a special committee involved with the church's new building decision, I laid it before the whole congregation as a possibility for me and for them.

Any church politician would have said enough's enough, and counseled me to forget the charismatic thing until the building business was all done.

The Beginnings in the Community

But new beginnings all came at once. God had seemed to give them all at once. And to back down on any of them seemed an unworthy and unfaithful retreat for me. So, we pressed on.

Very gradually, at first. The first evening teaching series. A few Sunday morning sermons. Open discussion of it with deacons and other "official family" who asked. An attempt to share it with the staff.

Praise God, the Spirit was moving in many places across our city and young people and middle-aged alike were having experiences of the Spirit in other places and bringing the joy back to Colonial.

A little midweek, and later Saturday morning, prayer group prayed week in and week out for the revival of the Spirit to come in Colonial. Over what now seems a very long time, their prayers were wonderfully answered.

The number of people baptized in the Spirit quietly grew in Colonial's life, aided by several times of breakthrough.

I had lain rather low for the first two or three years. It had seemed right. God seemed to be working quietly through our congregation in slowly leading a few people here and there in the ways of the Spirit.

Then one night in Lent, during a Sunday evening service, just before the sermon was to begin, the strange event that some had feared happened. Just as the hymn before the sermon concluded and the small congregation of perhaps one hundred and fifty people sat down, a young woman of the church remained standing and proceeded to speak in tongues. It was rather a loud and forceful voice.

I was stunned. And yet I felt God was in this, speaking to me and to the whole Colonial company. I was bent before the pulpit microphone and there softly praised God and thanked Jesus for the word to us. (Later these very words of praise and thanks of mine, which were recorded with the rest of that eventful service, were played as the final, accusing evidence that I had lost control of myself; they became the last and most convincing reason for one of my fellow workers to feel she'd had enough and to resign.)

As I began then to pray before the sermon another young woman, a friend of the first, gave what I assumed to be an interpretation of the tongues.

I preached the sermon, wondering all the while what my little congregation might be thinking. I did everything I could to incorporate that event into the total experience of the service and into my teaching in the sermon.

When it was over and we went downstairs for Lenten Supper the congregation was buzzing. The two young women were in one corner of the church praying with a little group that gathered around them. Another young woman I found prone on the floor, "slain in the Spirit." I feared the worst.

To my great surprise the congregation of that night was curious, interested, intrigued, wanting to know more, but not shocked. My own young son was eager to know what it was all about. "The sound was beautiful," he told his next older sister as she drove him home that evening. But neither of them understood what had happened.

I realized that night, there among my own five children,

that I had two generations of spiritual experiences. Clearly, I had some teaching and nurturing to do with my younger children—*and* with my whole congregation!

Even though I learned later that there was a strident urgency on the part of the two young women that came out of some emotional turmoil in the life of one of them, it was clear to me that God had used and wanted to use that event to remind me to get on with it—that there was a continuing revolution and revelation I must be about.

The following Sunday when a woman burst into tears and begged for prayer for healing during the little chancel communion following the regular morning worship services, I felt it was time for me to ask prayer in tongues. It was accepted in that little circle and welcomed, though reported later to others.

When Pentecost came that spring I was determined that we should celebrate it as the first Pentecost. It was Memorial Day Sunday. Many were away. I told the congregation we were going to celebrate it as nearly like the first Pentecost as we could. A young deacon came early in the morning and walked all around the church, praying blessing on that place and commanding the Evil One to have no part in that day. We sang folk songs, people shared prayers, we raised arms, I spoke in tongues and preached on the Spirit.

After each of the three services at least twenty-five people came forward to be prayed for for the baptism with the Holy Spirit. What tears, what hugging, what praise! There was even some tongues-speaking right there, loud and long, to the consternation of only a very few.

By nightfall the phone lines were hot. A number of church members indicated anger and fear. A few threatened to leave. Others were deeply blessed, and reported God's presence with them in wonderful new ways.

We had to live that down, but we were on our way. The next Pentecost Sunday was easier. And by the third year, people were eager for it, and coming because it was going to be a special Pentecost experience.

The Baptism Comes

In the fall of 1978 it seemed time to do some more evening teachings on the Holy Spirit. About one hundred came. A few were from other churches. We prayed and sang as well as taught.

Then the last night came. We sang and prayed and invited people who wanted the baptism to come forward. About twenty-five did. Did they receive it? I could scarcely tell. Until I heard of one young man, a high-school hockey star who, through the help of our young seminary student assistant, leaped into the air in joy and left the building praising God in tongues!

Another person stayed long afterward, I believe being humbled and broken by God until she literally could not stand. Confession and tears came as three of us ministered to her, and finally she received the release and freedom she longed for, and has been a radiant and beautiful witness among us ever since.

By springtime I was given opportunity to give the same series of talks on the Spirit to the people of the church in their regular Sunday morning learning communities. While there was no call to be baptized, there was a whole new spirit as we approached Pentecost this third year. People were ready. Forty or fifty came forward after each of two services. Report after report came back of people suddenly being filled with the Spirit, being healed of diseases and fears and literally finding new life.

What a joy! We were on our way! The baptism had at last become a regular and accepted part of our life.

Chapter 4

What Happened to Us as a Church?

IF you're a minister like me, and you hear a story about a church and an experience like this, especially in a day when there is so much tension and uncertainty about what the coming of the Holy Spirit might do to a safe and functioning congregation, you may say, "Yes, but what really happened? I mean, Arthur, you make it sound as if it just all worked out in the end—nice and easy. We've heard of churches that blew apart over the charismatic movement making inroads in their lives. We've heard of parishioners hurt and ministers fired and congregations divided. Didn't any of that happen to you? What price did you and Colonial really pay? What are the secrets, if any, that would help us open the way for the Spirit in our congregations? What happened to the conventional program? Who left? Who came? How did your staff react? What about influential lay leaders? Did anything happen to your peer-group relationships? What did the conference and the larger church think? What really happened inside that huge congregation? Tell us the story of how the son of a New England Congregational minister could get away with going to a more or less conventional middle western church of the Congregational tradition, seek and receive the baptism with the Holy Spirit, and continue to serve as the senior minister of that church without losing it all in the process? How did you and your people bring it off?"

Telling the true story is inevitably personal in a confessional sense and a matter of revealing those details known to and shared by the "family" of the congregation. It is my deep desire that nothing be said that would hurt any of those brothers and sisters of the way who are precious to me, to God, and to our whole Christian enterprise together. I will try to tell the truth of my own experience in this chapter in such a way as to preserve my own people and yet help my fellow church leaders to know the obstacles they might face, and the answers that came to help us through those tensions that the Spirit brought.

What Happened to the Conventional Program?

Colonial's senior deacon, my dear friend and brother, had asked me to write to the deacon board from my travels on sabbatical to tell them a little of what was happening to me. I did that sporadically, but it was enough to signal the church leaders that not only had I learned something, but that something had happened to me.

Some of them feared this, thinking it meant "Arthur will be different. He'll lay a new trip on us. He'll try to change us in some new way from what he's tried before. Colonial will never be the same again. He'll want us all to go into this emotional new thing. Wasn't it enough to put us through the John Kennedy assassination, and the racial-justice stuff, and the inner-city thing, and all the prayer business, and the Vietnam bit, and the anti-big-business themes without forcing us to follow him into this spooky religious emotionalism?"

In some ways the threat of the Spirit and all the assumptions and experiences they imagined to be part of it were worse than any of the social issues we had dealt with before, because receiving the Spirit is so intimately personal. Where you stood on that would not be just an issue "out there." It would be your own devotional life and personal experience of the faith.

There probably was a fear that the conventional program might be shoved aside and dismantled, and that we would become a different kind of church. Not that Colonial's program was what most people would have called conventional even then.

Colonial's power and interest for people in the late sixties and early seventies arose primarily from its being an enigma and an anachronism in the community. Some people wanted to see it as a "country club church." Its building in those days was, in fact, only a few blocks down the street from the Edina Country Club and all the senior ministers in town had been given honorary memberships in the club. In my earliest days in Edina it was clear that some people did want the church to be a club full of nice people, free in their understanding of Congregationalism to believe anything they wanted, and certainly not to have their economic and social principles of privilege and exclusiveness tampered with. It became evident that at least a few people wanted to tame the minister and pocket him as their own private chaplain. They would compliment him, and take him out to dinner, and tell him he was the greatest. But it became clear that the price was that he was not to challenge their prejudices—racial, economic, political, or social. They chided him about leaning too heavily on those issues. They felt early on that their new minister had no interest in being tamed or in having the church tamed—even though he loved and served and helped those people, and loves them to this day. They long since have left Colonial Church, taking their money and their invitations with them. But they are nonetheless loved and would be welcomed back into our life. I think they felt cheated of something—perhaps a control of the church they had hoped to have, or the luxury of a church and minister who would support their conservative economic and political ideas and commitments. These ideas and commitments, I gradually saw, were deeper and more ingrained than their faith commitment.

For a while they gently, and then obviously and publicly, ridiculed my positions and the symbolic things that stood out as galling to them in those midsixties days, like my longer hair and my jeans and boots. (I learned from an Edina police officer friend that in those days I was viewed by at least some on the force with condescension and disgust as "the hippie minister." Certainly that was the feeling, too, of some of the people of early importance in the church, and a source of frustration to them.)

Their initially-glowing prophecies that, with my abilities and preaching and the church's great potential, we would one day have a budget of a quarter of a million dollars, turned by the five-year mark into a dire prediction that people would leave in droves if I continued to press them on social issues and challenge them on Christian commitment—and, indeed, on repentance and new life.

It seemed to me very important to speak to the issues of the real life of people, and even to speak to some extent in the language of the day. The result was that one affluent, old-family lady huffed out of the church one day saying, "I don't want any more of that sin, sex, and slang!" She never came back.

So the perception of the style and form of ministry we were carrying on was not that it was conventional. We tried to be very direct with people: to laugh a lot, to let church be fun, to clap in church, to meet people where they were, and to love them. I'd like to think our program reflected that.

While we did lots of the usual conventional things, like sponsoring a Boy Scout troop and a Cub pack, housing some Girl Scout troops, and having a women's bazaar and a Women's Fellowship, there were other approaches to the program that were somewhat different.

Our approach to staff was different. I had failed early on with assistants, and so the church joined me in seeking a staff of specialists. They were expert in what they did and ran their own programs. We called an administrator-coordinator, who did organizing, money, fund-raising, and coordinating of committees. We called a teaching minister, skilled in theology and the Bible. He initiated Bible studies and other forms of study at a consistently deeper level than would normally have been possible—than I alone had been able to do.

We called a youth director, but assigned half his time to working with kids "out there" in the community. He helped establish Young Life in the town and was one of its leaders, even while he led the church's own high school Pilgrim Fellowship. He instituted spring vacation ski trips for PF that became high times in the Spirit. He trained laypeople to work as counselors and leaders in the community's Young Life ministry. As a church, Colonial tried to respond to the needs of kids in those early 1960s. We helped establish a high-school teen center. Later we housed a weekly Friday night junior-high dance. Out of this came The Colony, with a ministry to youngsters lonely and not making it. Then Colonial birthed "Reborn"—a teenage AA group. Trips became a regular part of our approach with canoeing in Minnesota's north country and talks of faith around the fire, and other trips to Chicago's inner city for a long weekend of cleanup help there. Summer missions trips were part of the youth ministry as well.

The youth minister later became a skilled counseling minister as the church tried to respond to the breakdown in individual and family life. His ministry developed women's support groups and, through the 1970s, grief support and job-transition support groups have grown.

My own work was perhaps the most conventional in that I preached, made hospital calls twice a week, visited people in their homes. But during the sixties especially, I made a point of ministering to men by taking one afternoon each week to call on them in their offices and factories, and by leading twelve monthly men's luncheon discussion groups that dealt with all the raging issues of those turbulent years. These groups, in fact, were the key to our survival as a church through those years. The angry and dismayed men were at least coming face to face with their minister in groups of six to fifteen and talking once a month. They at least knew their minister loved them and was sincere in his convictions—even while they clearly disagreed with him. It was a vital pastoral contact.

With women I was investing time helping them with Days Away and Schools of Prayer and the development of a "prayer chain" of seventy women who committed themselves to daily intercessory prayer for a long list of people in need.

We were also praying for the sick and the grieving by name, and for other personal and world needs, in the pastoral prayer each Sunday.

We were becoming heavily involved in mission during those years, investing ourselves in the inner city, and on Indian reservations, and in a number of vital missions around the world. The giving of 25 percent of our total budget to missions became a sacred moral principle. We were trying to reach out, and to serve. In the late sixties we

established a daily phone message of faith and encouragement. We became involved in the world of an international medical mission called Project Concern and many
of us have annually walked the thirty kilometers of its
"Walk for Mankind" to raise funds for its work.

So all through the 1960s assumptions were being built
in the mind and spirit of the church: that we were a missionary church; that we loved all people and certainly
young people; that we were prepared to give ourselves
away as a church in serving the community without expect-
ing any payment or favors in return; that we'd do anything
we could to meet a need that surfaced in the community;
that we were a praying people; that we believed Christ
answers prayer and does heal the sick, and make the blind
see, and the lame walk; that we were committed to Christ
most of all and to loving one another, even though we
disagreed. We assumed a commitment to social change, to
Bible study, to developing a program flexible enough to
respond to what was happening to people.

One would think such a program would be a good base
and foundation for a new experience for the church of the
Holy Spirit. Part of me felt my flock would be ready for
anything—that they had become a loose, flexible, faithful
crowd. And they were.

The charismatic, Holy Spirit idea stirs deep feelings and
passions, touches deep roots in the hearts of people. Many
of the people, I found, had had very early experiences of
old-line fundamental faith with various rigidites and vocal
expressions of emotion. They feared I might be taking
them back to that. They feared the good things that had
happened in Colonial Church might be destroyed. If I was
different they felt sure they would be asked to be different.

[47]

They feared, I think, that our worship would change, that it would become more emotional, less controlled, perhaps longer and less structured than it was.

Some clearly believed I would cease to care about social justice and would influence the church's program in the direction of just a lot of prayer and singing and the exercise of strange gifts like speaking in tongues. They may have felt I would be tempted to become an Aimee Semple Mc-Pherson, and would be like the emerging television preachers, and would do more ranting and raving than I had done.

They feared more a philosophical change in the general direction of the church than that specific programs would change. They feared I would change and that they would be asked to change.

My own assumption was that we had already grown into a loving community of faith, which was part of my reason for taking the sabbatical tour to see what else the Spirit was doing "out there." I felt we were already a somewhat carefree crowd, and that we had built up enough of a trust for one another so that they would know I would still be committed to all the emphases of the past even though new dimensions would be brought to our life.

It was dismaying to me that they felt they had any need to worry. My mistake was to think that whatever they might feel about any new theological or spiritual emphasis I might bring back to them, they would know that the delicate balance of passions and concerns, which I deeply shared with them, could be assumed to be safe and inviolate.

In fact, as I look back now over the ten years since the sabbatical pilgrimage and my baptism with the Holy Spirit, I can see that indeed there have been some changes even in our already unconventional program. Probably those changes and additions could not have come and become permanent in our life had not the original program and ministry already been there. Nor could they have come about without the commitment of the staff and lay leaders to experimentation and a sense and style of freedom.

The acceptance of the Holy Spirit experience could happen and become part of the church's program because of the foundations that had already inadvertently been laid.

What changed? Worship did. My own modest research uncovered the fact that late Puritan worship in the colonies at the time of the American Revolution had several marks not unlike those that characterize the worship of the modern charismatics and Pentecostals. They early on had an almost ritual loving greeting of one another, a kind of "passing of the peace." For the opening prayer the people stood with hands raised above their heads. They also sang hymns in a free, a cappella way.

So one area of change was to invite the people to greet each other after the opening welcome, which now they do with delight and eagerness and with hugs and handshakes and expressions of welcome and love to everyone around them. The ministers leave the platform and move among the nearer people, greeting them in the same way.

Then a minister raises his or her arms, and invites the people to do so, in prayer—"as our Pilgrim and Puritan forebears did" (not "as the Pentecostals" do!)—and most of the congregation willingly and eagerly do so. Because the Congregational way is theologically a Holy Spirit way with a high doctrine of the place and power of the Holy Spirit, this became a very natural tie for us. Our formal public worship then, has taken on a kind of Holy Spirit/ Pilgrim character: almost a modern Spirit/Pilgrim liturgy.

Another part of the program was teaching. I set out to

do some specific teaching on the Holy Spirit. At first it was a series of "teachings by Arthur" at a time different from other programs: like five consecutive Wednesday evenings the first year, and four Advent Sunday evenings five years later, and finally three different four-week series in our Sunday morning learning communities.

The earlier series climaxed in an invitation to come forward to receive the baptism. Singing accompanied this praying with laying on of hands. It became a kind of wonderful, free worship. Many responded and were "filled with the Holy Spirit."

That teaching on the Spirit and offering prayer for healing, receiving the Spirit, or other help has become the pattern for a 6 p.m. Sunday "agape" service which, though small in numbers, has come to fill a large place in the lives of a few people. At the end of this easy, blue-jeaned, relaxed, Spirit-singing and Spirit-praying service, carried on in the round in front of the fireplace in our "hearth room," a few cushions are laid on the floor, usually by one of the people, the minister or ministers kneel beside the cushions, and while the group sings softly, those with special needs for themselves or others come and kneel and are touched or held and prayed for by the ministers—often with two or three other people from the circle of twenty-five or thirty coming to lay hands in love upon the person from behind, and to join in the prayers.

Pentecost Sunday for the last five or six years has been celebrated with shared prayers, speaking in tongues by the minister and some of the people in prayer, by guitar-accompanied singing, and by other freer elements in worship, climaxed by invitations to those who wish to come forward for prayer for the baptism in their life. Perhaps two hundred people responded in 1980 out of two congregations, which on that Memorial Day weekend numbered a little over nine hundred; and another one hundred or more on a baccalaureate on Pentecost Sunday in 1981 with over twelve hundred present in the congregation. There were tears, tongues, healings, and the gift of new direction of life for most of those people. In worship, the Holy Spirit sense and place is here to stay. This, I think, is widely agreed upon by our people.

A change that has come in our counseling program is that our counseling minister himself has felt freer to use the disciplines of the "healing of the memories" and the whole area of "inner healing." The laypeople trained to do marriage and other counseling are probably freer to pray with the people they see, and freer to share their own lives as a result of the greater openness and awareness to the Spirit's presence and power that has come to us.

The high school Pilgrim Fellowship, both in its large Sunday evening meeting, but especially in its smaller discipling groups, has felt an encouragement and a legitimizing of the expression of charismatic elements in prayer and attitude. Tongues are spoken softly, kids are open to the Spirit experience, and the freedom that was already there has been enhanced and expanded because the young people have felt that was OK with the church—that the church people were with them in all that.

A naturalness to the flow of the Spirit in all aspects of the church's life and program has increased in the past six or eight years and cannot be unrelated to the teaching on the Spirit that has been brought to the church, both in special teaching sessions and in considerable teaching through sermons.

We may even have become more open to financially supporting and sharing in some missions that are of a more charismatic character than those we might have supported previous to the invasion of the Spirit in our life. Clearly the program has been affected by this new experience in our life as a church.

Who Left?

When I hear the story of a major change coming in a church's life, a dramatic shift in emphasis, a concerned and serious attempt at renewal, I instinctively wonder: What was the price? What was the cost of this gain? Were members or money lost? Did the church fold? Or was there something strong enough in what was brought to the church in the new gifts and emphases that enabled the church to survive the jar and the shock?

Did anybody leave Colonial Church when the minister returned with his new vision and experience of the Spirit? The answer is yes. Lots? Relatively few. People have left Colonial Church for a variety of reasons over the years, and in protest over various issues. Some write a letter expressing their displeasure, others ask for a luncheon or other interview with the minister for purposes of stating their displeasure—sometimes in the hope that I would change, but more often to state clearly the fact of their departure and the reason for it.

Most people who leave, in my experience, just fade away. They may indeed be angry. They may hope they will be missed and that their departure will have an impact. But if it causes no stir they will take that as a sign that we are a callous and uncaring church, and good riddance that they are free of us. Once a woman wrote me after having taken steps to have her name removed from our rolls, saying: "Praise God! At last the ill A. Rouner no longer has a hold over our family!" She had been deeply hurt by a misunderstanding that colored her whole view of the church and the minister. She could see us in only the worst possible terms.

People have many expectations of churches. They may develop a close relation with the minister or ministers. I find that sometimes that leads them to feel they have a certain authority with him (or her): they can, if not control the minister, at least have his ear in a special way. Then if in a sermon or pastoral letter or at a board meeting that minister takes a position contrary to the one they've expressed to him and perhaps pressed on him, a rift is created and they feel done in, diddled out of some sort of hope for authority, and, taking the only noticeable action left to them, they leave in the proverbial huff.

As we encouraged people in worship to raise hands in prayer to God, or to hold hands at the end of each service, rumblings did come back of the displeasure of some people—people who didn't even want to hold hands with their own family in church.

One of my own college-age children chided me a year or two ago for inviting everybody to hug a father in the congregation on Father's Day. She found it an embarrassment at that stage of her life to reach out with that degree of intimacy to some father figure down the row who wasn't already known to her.

A few people with these kinds of feelings doubtless left us, as did some who simply would not let their worst fears be assuaged. And yet many stuck it out and stayed and have learned to tolerate and even love the new, freer, and more openly loving character that has come to dominate their church's life.

Again, the old experiences of highly-charged fundamentalist or Pentecostal worship in early childhood and feelings of being confused and emotionally overwhelmed in those early years came back too powerfully to be resisted for some, and they could not afford, psychically or spiritually, to wait and see what really would happen in the church home they had found at Colonial. The unresolved and unhealed hurts of earlier experiences were just too frightening to allow them the freedom to wait and see, and even to be fair in evaluation, which their otherwise more normal adult balance would have made possible.

To my knowledge, the ones who left early on just disappeared. For others, departure was the result of a cumulative disappointment over a variety of "new" factors in the life of the church they loved.

One man came one night to say he and his wife had been visiting the local Presbyterian church for the last six months and the next Sunday they would be joining. He went on to say how they had decided in their recent retirement not to go to Phoenix, but had stayed in Edina primarily because of their love for the church.

Note here that they had already endured for over sixteen years the crises the church had gone through, particularly on social action issues, since I had come. They had believed in the emphasis on human justice. They hadn't been turned away by the economic critiques from the pulpit. But "something's different," he said. "There's no quiet in the church anymore. No silence before worship. No respect."

It was the freedom of people to greet each other, to reach out in love—which had grown rather noisy—that at least symbolized to that older couple "the trouble with the new Colonial." In fact, they had opposed the buying of new property and the building of a new church. But the charismatic Holy Spirit elements had become part of the new equation that bothered them, and finally made intolerable this church that had meant so much to them.

Another older man made the same move away to the same neighboring church. He, too, had ridden out many of the storms. He had served on an important board of the church. He was of gentle heart, a lover of the hymns and all the music he found at Colonial. But when he left in 1978 he said, "it's just gotten to be too much for me. I'm not in tune with Colonial anymore." But hints dropped to other people suggested that two factors were working negatively to do him in at Colonial. One was that our summer preacher the previous summer had been a black Baptist from a sister church of Colonial's in the city. Many of that minister's people had come along to share in the worship at Colonial. So had the preacher's wife. She had sat in the front row. She made it an amen corner. "Right on! Tell 'em. Yes!! Preach it!" and such other appropriate Baptist comments of encouragement peppered the response to his preaching from his wife and from his flock.

The black Baptists brought together two elements that were just too hard for this older man: black people and his own feelings of uncertainty and perhaps fear of them, and their emotionalism, which he evidently feared was coming now to his Colonial. Together, they did him in.

But, Who Came?

The traffic was not all one way. In the late 1960s people began coming to Colonial Church because it was a church that had declared itself as opposed to racial discrimination in church membership, and supportive of conscientious objection to war, and because the church had extended itself to help the inner city and to act with compassion there.

By 1967 and 1968 there was a definite turning of the tide. Members in their fifties, a vital age group of Minneapolis leadership who had given financial help as well as other leadership to the church, had either dropped away or sat on their hands in the mid-1960s. It was an unhealthy loss for the church.

But then new, younger people with small children began coming in greater and greater numbers—*because* the church was active and involved in social issues, because it was trying to change the city, because it did seem to understand and care about poverty and delinquency and alcoholism, and because it opposed both racial prejudice and war.

These young people were on the rise in their businesses. They had come to live in Edina. But they were very troubled by the pressures of affluence and success. In their hearts they were more politically and economically liberal than many of the older people around them in their safe and lovely neighborhoods. The church became a beacon of encouragement to them in their yearning not to be typical suburbanites with not a care for the poor and the hurt of the world.

Some of them had come from either fundamentalist churches that seemed to have little social conscience or from liberal churches that had only social conscience and no real God, no live Christ. In both cases they yearned to be involved in the world, but they wanted to go to it with the presence and love of a living Christ.

Curiously, these excited young people gradually began to introduce their own parents to Colonial Church. They were people of the same age as the older, established church members we had begun to lose. Now suddenly there came, in this whole new way, an entirely different set of established fifty- to sixty-five-year-old grandparently people whose strength and support we greatly needed. It was an answer to prayer—a critically important gift of life to Colonial Church.

That was in the late 1960s and early seventies.

What had happened then began to happen again in the mid- to late 1970s. Not in spite of this strange mixture we had become as a church, but because of it, began to come this whole new group of people.

They were the hurting, the new lonely, the divorced, the widowed, the angry, the wounded: the people who turned inward in the seventies and saw emptiness there, and longing, and resentment, and hurt. They began coming because the church began speaking more and more in a confessional way to those issues, those wounds of society.

The prayer services were there at Colonial. Pentecost was celebrated with real gifts of the Spirit. Real healing took place in the lives of people. The new Colonial people were serious about prayer. This was the place for them. They came because of what we had become, because some of us, at least, spoke in tongues, healed, prophesied, taught with a mind open to the Spirit. Because we expected miracles. Because we dared to risk financially the building of a three-and-a-half-million-dollar building and to march as a company one thousand strong to occupy the new land and be a mission place, a "city set upon a hill." The books I wrote during the seventies reflect this change. They were on prayer, on love, on marriage, and on healing.

Folks were wanting that—along with the social change ministries, and the deepened biblical study. There was love here, and healing: what one woman called "Colonial curbside service"—which meant an arm thrown around you and a prayer offered for you right on the spot, by ministers or laypeople, if you were found weeping after church or asking for help.

So the loose, Spirit-centered, occasional Sunday morning altar-calling, and evening service healing, and prayer-believing spirit of this increasingly loving church began to be the reason for a whole new group of people coming to Colonial Church. They were glad to know the senior minister was baptized in the Spirit and prays for healing. To them that was a positive, not a negative.

And who were these folks? Mr. Gallup's American unchurched: the people who'd been gone from the Christian church for a decade, turned off by some lack of caring, or oppressive traditionalism, or something "way back when." Now their experience is turning them back toward the church, and maybe to a different, freer, more seeking and open church tradition than the one from which they had come.

Thus, the new-members classes being received by Colonial Church in the new building—even in a very family-centered suburb—are made up frequently of one-third Roman Catholics by background, and out of some sixty people, are forty single people (mostly divorced, but some widowed or never married), and only ten couples.

We are serving a new kind of constituency. Not just because we are in a more mission-oriented stance on a major crosstown highway, not just because we have a new building. But partly because our society—a society that is perceptibly changing in its makeup, that is feeling the pain of divorce and all its trauma and rejection, and that is the victim (and cause) of other kinds of disruptions—is now on a new search for meaning. The searchers have learned that they have emotions, they have a heart, they need other people, they want to be touched and hugged and healed and lifted out of themselves in praise, and song, and, yes, maybe even in the freeing utterance of tongues of praise.

The Spirit experience and charismatic movement in Colonial Church has had a significant part in drawing this new, hurting, seeking constituency into our life.

How Did the Staff React?

The staff reacted with bemusement, suspicion, some feeling of being threatened, some curiosity, and even some eagerness as time went on.

The staff consisted at that time of seven full-time professional people. There was also a support group of perhaps five or six secretaries. A music staff included four people part-time. Beyond them was a crew of three or four part-time custodians.

One of the most curious aspects of the staff's whole reaction was the emergence of a very particular reaction growing out of specific childhood experiences in the conservative Baptist tradition.

Four young people on our staff were highly gifted people, two of whom had grown up in ministers' families in the "Conference" Baptist tradition. All four of them were in the process of a kind of pilgrimage of their own, in a liberalizing, freeing direction. Colonial had been a wonderful way station for them spiritually, where the old rigidities and legalisms were gone, but the living Christ was real and lifted up and followed. They were also eager for social concern to change the world as well as to change individual people—all of which they found at Colonial Church.

One of them was a highly-trained biblical scholar of impeccable European scholastic credentials. He had scholarly and intellectual concerns to deal with in the whole Pentecostal, Spirit business. But he had grown up in church in the back "hollers" of West Virginia, where his father had been a minister of small Baptist churches. There he had witnessed as a child the strange performances, by some of the very simple, literalist, Christian hill folk, of snake-handling and poison-drinking that were crude ways of proving great faith (based on the Pauline protest that none of those enemies could hurt the believer in Christ).

He knew of simple people who had died as a result of such excesses, so he had good reason for caution as his preaching colleague came back full of the enthusiasm of his Spirit experience, and with the obvious desire to pass it on to the congregation.

But more than that, the three others, however liberated they had thought they were, found they had deep inside them an instinctive resistance to the implications of the whole Pentecost story in Acts and the implications coming from it for the church today.

For they had been brought up in their Baptist tradition to believe there was a special dispensation given by God to the apostles. Once the church had been birthed in the Spirit, and had received the power Jesus had promised, that Spirit would be withdrawn from all those generations to follow the apostolic period simply because the "roaring mighty wind" and flames of fire and unknown tongues wouldn't be needed. The Spirit, in the view of Dispensationalism, was an experience given only to the apostolic community, really just to get the church started.

Implied in that doctrine's teaching, was a certain sense of danger about the Spirit. The Spirit was too unpredictable. The Bible, however, was safer, contained on pages and between covers, and that was the only authority. That biblicist understanding really put the Bible above the Spirit, and also above God, the divine Self.

While these sharp young people on Colonial's staff had

put much of their early beginnings behind them, and certainly felt that they had outgrown everything narrow and judgmental in their spiritual background, they surprised themselves to discover how powerful, from their early Baptist teaching, was dispensational theology still in their own theological assumptions.

I do not think this made them skeptical or brought any rigid refusal to go along. It just brought caution, a desire to hear the whole story from me, and time to work through for themselves how far they could go in accepting such an experience for their own ministry.

Some on the staff were trusting enough to assume that if I had had the experience, and felt I had a theological and biblical use for it, then it must be OK. While they weren't seeking it for themselves, they were willing that it be my experience, and part of my teaching in the church.

For one of us it was harder because my experience seemed to imply that now there was a judgment coming from me that only Christians who had had the Spirit experience were really Christians and that Christians—and especially ministers—had better get on to having the experience. I think he resisted anything that implied that there was any further stage for Christians, any new experience, different from what one already had in being baptized and originally giving one's heart to Christ.

In fact, most ministers resist the Spirit experience and idea because if they accept it, then logically they must do something about it. It inevitably calls them to a new pilgrimage, a new search of their own. And most of us who have been ministers for a decade or two, have so much invested in our hard-won answers to our own questions of faith, that the idea of starting over, and learning—like a little child—a whole new aspect of the Christian experience, seems both like too much work and like having to admit that one hadn't actually "had it all together" and there was more to learn.

Perhaps the whole Christian experience is a lifetime of pilgrimage, and growth, and stages, and new learnings, and again and again and again humblings of the ego and consequent new beginnings. Indeed, it had been exactly so for me. The very experience of receiving the Spirit and speaking in tongues had been increasingly embarrassing as I came close to the moment of the new baptism. I realized I was going to lose a power of speech, a care for words, a control of the voice and of saying exactly what I wanted to say—a peculiarly preacherly concern.

I had feared to let go. After I did, and the joy came, and the new freedom grew, I realized there was a whole new thing I had to learn: that I, the mature, more or less skilled and apparently successful suburban minister, had to begin all over again. I had to read the scriptures in a whole new way and had to account for a new dimension in the New Testament—the Holy Spirit, the promise of the Spirit, the presence of the Spirit, right there in Jesus' teaching, primary in that for which Jesus was preparing his disciples: the ministry of power he had called them to, and promised them. Everywhere "Holy Spirit" leaped out at me as I read the New Testament through again.

If I was to teach my people I would have to be a child again, a babe, keeping only a step ahead of the flock in passing on to them the new truth I was learning as I went.

Of course, it was a humbling experience. Yes, it was hard to admit that here was something out of the heart of the gospel that I was just now learning as a middle-aged Christian and minister.

So I had sympathy for my brothers and sisters of the staff who resisted at first, quite naturally, what could imply real change for their own lives, as well as for the life of Colonial Church as a Christian company.

None of the staff doffed his or her robes in public worship and walked out on me. No one tried to lead a floor fight against the funny new thing Arthur had brought to the church. However, I could hardly have expected them to roll over and die and say, "Anything you say, Arthur. If you're for the Spirit, we'll all buy it too." They never were that kind of staff. All individuals, all strong leaders, all scripture students and theologians in their own right, they would accept this experience, this view of the scripture and its message only as they searched it through themselves and could make it their own.

Gradually they did make it their own. For the first two or three years there was a tendency to pass off the Spirit experience, the Spirit people, and the Spirit days, like Pentecost, as "Arthur's thing—something we tolerate, but don't get too excited about." But slowly that changed. Some turnover has come in the staff. Some of the young staff members found their own constituency—like the church's youth—open to the Spirit and asking about receiving it. Over the ten years since 1972 it became easier for Colonial's ministerial staff to be open to the Spirit, to accept it, and finally to encourage it. Now, after a long decade, all of them share in leading Pentecost worship services. They themselves are willing to meet the people flocking forward at the end of the services and to lay hands on them in love and to pray for the baptism of the Spirit upon those who come from all the diverse elements within our congregation.

My ministerial colleagues could hardly help being caught up in the power of the experience on the Day of Pentecost these past few years. Their own growth and acceptance has been gradual, but perceptive and real. Those

who had not had a high view of prayer as a power for healing have begun ministering in a healing way in the informal evening "agape" services. Gradually the
theological ideas and biblical base for the Spirit position
have been more easily accepted by them all. The openness
of almost all our younger seminary assistants to the Spirit
power and ministry has encouraged the professional staff.

They still have their cautions, but year by year it
becomes a more natural part of the church's life for them.
Our love and unity have grown, and the Spirit assumptions have been largely accepted.

One interesting staff member who at times might not
have seemed a personality as likely to be open to the Spirit
and to hands-laying, and praying, and long meetings with
"altar calls" and other such manifestations of emotion
generally assumed to be alien to our tradition, has been
our gifted young organist-composer, a professor of music
and now a department chairman at one of the country's
fine undergraduate music colleges. Though he is steeped
in classical music, with a Ph.D. in music theory and com-
position, the breadth of his understanding of worship in-
cludes a place for freedom, and expression of deep feeling
and a very personal love for Jesus. To some extent this was
born out of a time of personal heartache and need when it
was the faith that brought him through. His contribution
to the struggle to open the Colonial Church people to the
Spirit was a surprisingly personal openness combined with
the gift of a high-quality musicianship that became a very
positive support.

He was the one who, from the beginning, was ready to
play background music on the organ as weeping people
were prayed for, and several times went out with me in an
almost Moody and Sankey routine to lead healing services—in one instance for the national group of Congrega-

tionalists gathered in annual meeting—playing the old hymns and supporting me on the piano for what seemed hours, as people came forward for prayer.

What more could one ask from a highly-trained, creative, individualistic, but committed and faithful staff of colleagues in ministry? It could have gone very differently. They could have sowed the seeds of discord. They could have undercut me and our common enterprise. But somehow God allowed us to grow together, accepting one another, and giving to one another the gift of time and space so that our common pilgrimage could take place.

What About Influential Lay Leaders?

My brother and sister leaders of the church began, I think, with a feeling of some responsibility for what had happened to me. They had made an investment in this sabbatical with which they were rewarding me for ten years of service to them. They had raised money as a gift to help my wife and children join me for the European part of the tour. They had given me jeans, shirts, and kerchiefs for my western travels. They were intrigued with the idea of this way of studying and learning. To a real extent, it was their deal.

I don't think they were embarrassed. They read in my letters back to them what had happened. Several women deacons put two and two together, saw that the Lutheran charismatic conference was coming to town during August while I was still away, and that if they were going to understand this thing that had happened to Arthur, they had better get on down there and find out what it was about. And they did.

Several of them waited for me soon after my return to try to understand the experience, but also to voice their apprehensions about what this might mean for the church. Would they all be under judgment now? Did I think everybody had to have the Spirit experience in order to be a Christian? How would the church be different? How would I be different?

They needed reassurance. I did everything I could to give it to them. I was the same man who left them four months before. I was still committed to all the basic things that had characterized my life and our ministry together in the past. I still loved them. I was not about to browbeat them with this thing. But I had learned something new to me, and vital for the church, and, yes, I did want to share it with them all as time went on and they were able to receive it.

In the year before the sabbatical we had brought charismatic Catholic people in to address a number of our groups of men and women. The church leaders had at least some inkling of my interest and concern. The experience had not come without some warning.

The church's leaders asked me to do some teaching. My first four sermons of the fall described the whole sabbatical and its meaning for me. At the same time, five Wednesday evening teachings by me on the Holy Spirit drew about one hundred people, some of whom were church officers. Several backed off and said they just weren't ready yet for that.

One brilliant young scientist found Christ there, received the baptism with the Spirit the last night, and went on to become a deacon and later senior deacon of the church. He was an utterly sincere man but one who had not cared about faith. He had been engrossed in his biological research and had been hesitant and shy in his relations with people. But he had begun to be a seeker, and he came looking to those meetings. What was exciting was how much he found and how greatly he changed in personality and commitment. He has become a loving brother to many in the community, and has set about quietly to pass on his growing faith to his children and his wife, and to many groping and troubled people. He has become a skilled teacher, a wonderfully patient and humble father, and a supportive and effectively ministering lay leader in the church.

Already a core of people in the church, through prayer groups and Bible studies had come into the experience of the Spirit. They prayed for us all—for the staff and the leaders. More and more—the deaconly people especially— came on their own into the Spirit experience. Other church officers held back.

Only one man clearly made a point of protest, probably a year or two after that fall of 1972, dramatically resigning his office as a deacon because of the Spirit direction he saw the church taking—particularly the lifting up of hands in prayer during public worship. In self-defense he threatened to leave if it happened again. It did, and he stayed. He was frequently critical, I would say, but a committed comrade who remains a friend and still contributes in wonderfully positive ways to the strengthening and growth of the church's life. I believe that a quality of love that the Spirit creates in a congregation is what has kept this man and others like him in the church and still open in spite of their fears and reservations.

On the other side was a true old-timer, a crusty lawyer (he'd say that of himself) and labor negotiator who stuck with the church through thick and thin when many others had abandoned it. He came storming up out of the congregation one Sunday immediately after the service because we had invited those who would like to "follow Jesus" to stand during the last hymn, but had forgotten to invite the rest of the congregation—as is our custom—to stand and hold hands as brothers and sisters for the benediction. He felt put down because he had *not* been allowed to give physical expression to the Spirit of God in his life! A good Democrat-Liberal, my dear friend, a man of conscience, who had always been acceptable to whatever "old guard" there might be, but whose heart was right there with the new thing and the true faith.

That stands as a sign to me of where those "prominent lay leaders" were when the time for accounting came. They stood together—in support.

Did Anything Happen to the Peer Group Relationships?

What about the brother and sister ministers "out there" in the community and in the country? Were they dismayed? Did they abandon me? Did they back off and sit looser in their friendships with me? Did I become anathema to some? Was my reputation, such as it was, harmed or helped?

A number of things happened in my life as a minister as a result of my Spirit experience. Over the years those results, I realize now, have affected in several different ways my peer relationships.

The experience of baptism with the Holy Spirit was, in the first place, a freeing experience for me. It freed me, I do believe, from any pompous pretensions I may formerly have had. Less and less did I have a sense of being a successful suburban minister who could produce a comforting, caring funeral service, or a joyful, personal wedding service on short notice. I came to worry less about how I was doing. I feel I was given an ability or a gift of being able to carry on with hope even when I was not able to feel a great deal of joy.

A great deal of work had already been done to lift me from an earlier time of despondency and sin and broken-heartedness in my life when I had been just hanging on to my ministry, marriage, and meaning in life. I had found the way, through the forgiveness of Christ. I was set free to love. My own ministry had become more loving. Consequently, I believe, my own congregation was freed to love and did grow immensely as a loving company of faith. Their love was the reason for the peculiar search for the Spirit, through the sabbatical pilgrimage, in the first place.

A group of ministerial colleagues in those days some dozen years ago knew of my struggles, had prayed for me, and had specifically gathered round and laid hands upon me for the receiving of the Spirit. They were not all still in town when it finally happened for me five years later. But, without question, they rejoiced for me, understood my need for that experience of faith, and continued to love me. They, at least, saw that experience as a sign of growth for me and welcomed it. They continue to be long-distance friends, occasional correspondents, and, I believe, partners and brothers in prayer.

But the new freedom and humbling of the charismatic experience opened me to take bigger chances in the ministry. I think it prepared the way for me to find a new toughness and resilience as the leader of a large congregation, and to be more able to take the battles and beatings and antagonisms and grief that are an inevitable part of the responsibility of the senior pastor in the large church, or, for that matter, in any size church.

I realize only now that in the years since 1972 I have had more occasions when it seemed necessary to take great risks in certain struggles within the life and leadership of the church. I have been more ready to take public stands in the broad community that involved risk to me. In some instances those positions made me appear to be more of a social conservative than I am, in the eyes of my liberal clerical colleagues, particularly in the United Church of Christ side of American Congregationalism.

This has been most noticeable with some of my fellow ministers of the larger United Church of Christ churches in my own towns of Minneapolis and St. Paul. This has been a particular regret to me because, although I have tried to be present at many conference and association gatherings, the demands of my own parish responsibilities have limited the opportunities for brotherly and sisterly exchange and friendship with those colleagues.

The privilege came to me in 1978 of serving on a new "board of contributors" of the large evening newspaper of Minneapolis, *The Minneapolis Star*. The paper wanted "opinion." I gave it to them frequently, in articles that grew out of both pastoral letters to my own congregation and community concerns that were important to me.

I took positions in opposition to abortion, in criticism of the widely held view that "separation of church and state" means no religion of any kind expressed in any public way in civil life generally or in public-school life particularly. I have been critical of prevailing moral standards in sex and marriage, in drug abuse and alcoholism, in civil and corporate ethics.

Curious to me is how this, combined with my perceived evangelicalism in state conference and association circles, has served, within a scant year or two, to turn the attitude of two or three brother ministers from perhaps grudging acceptance of my denominational nonconformity, and tolerant curiosity at the apparent success in Colonial Church's growth in membership and money, to disparagement in a couple of instances from men who had only a year earlier gone out of their way to be personally cordial.

At a Florida consultation of United Church of Christ ministers of the denomination's larger churches, one of my colleagues, referring to a conversation in which another minister had stated that he and I had been "talking theology," shot back: "Theology with Arthur Rouner? I didn't know he had any theology from what he's putting out in the papers!"

Prior to my Holy Spirit experience I might not have felt free to write "in the papers" some of the things I believed were important to say. Of course, I like to be understood and approved by my denominational colleagues and might not have dared to risk the loss of whatever approval I had.

Jesus says that the Spirit will give us the words to say in a time of testing and I believe that has happened for me, and will happen for anyone who seeks the Spirit's power and help. It is certainly not that I do not care about the opinions of my colleagues. But I have felt freer to take the risk of doing the more difficult and needed public thing— namely, to try to deal with the subtleties of the highly emotional issues that have become such an important part of our politics.

As the husband of a working wife, and the father of a daughter preparing for the ministry, it has seemed impor-tant to be candid and honest about the issues that feminists raise and to differ with them where I feel I had to with as much grace and sensitivity as I can. The "sexual revolution" has wrought considerable havoc with a lot of lives that I see pastorally. Speaking out from that position does not tend to make one popular today.

I'd simply found I was more prepared to say what I believed, and to ride out the storm of any losses of friend-ship I might incur. This has been a direct result of my ex-perience with the Holy Spirit.

[71]

The other side of it is that many other ministers have admired my willingness to be open to being caught and claimed and changed by the Holy Spirit. I have become more interesting to them. Two UCC senior ministers have even come to visit Colonial Church for long weekends—presumably to observe the ministry they sense is happening in the community through Colonial since the days of our awakening to the Spirit. I believe these two men have perceived that something of significance is at work in our life and that it may well be born of the Spirit, and they want to know about that. With these people our Spirit experience has become an advantage and has given me a new credibility and some approval with my colleagues.

In one instance, during a very difficult time at Colonial Church while we were in the throes of heavy decisions about whether to move and build a new church, I met several times with the pastoral search committee of a large congregation of the United Church of Christ. They voted to call me to be their candidate for senior minister of their denominational church. What was fascinating to me was their answer when I confessed to them my passionate commitments to social change and my charismatic experience and pastoral commitment to a ministry of Christian healing and use of spiritual gifts for me and the people in any church I might serve.

"We know all about that," they said, "we've checked you out, and none of that bothers us." That congregation saw its own need, and identified the Spirit's gifts in Colonial's ministry as something not to be feared, but welcomed.

To that degree they were probably ahead of many of my United Church of Christ ministerial colleagues at that time. Indeed, one Union Seminary professor serving on the ministerial standing committee of the New York City

Association which included this church, reported to the committee chairman that, in traveling through Minneapolis he had inquired into my reputation and was informed of the charismatic and social gospel concerns of my ministry, and of my generally evangelical theology. He evidently viewed this information as a distinct negative.

Interestingly, in the years since, a strong Fellowship of Charismatic Christians is growing within the United Church of Christ, embracing some of its most famous social activists, who have gained positive acceptance. The National Association of Congregational Christians (the other side of Colonial Church's denominational heritage) is likewise seeing a growth in its ranks of evangelicals and charismatics among its newer and younger clergy and laypeople.

This fact tends to make me, as an "older" minister who is widely known to have had the charismatic experience, a rather more interesting and intriguing colleague than before. Now there is a sort of survival factor surrounding me—a sense even of some mystery—in that I have been able to go through the charismatic experience personally, deliberately share it in teaching and preaching with my congregation, and still not only hold onto my job, but have enabled the church to grow and expand and reach out, and even build a new and expensive building during that very same period.

The ministers of other large churches have been by far the most sympathetic colleagues in the ministry to my charismatic experience. They are the ones who know something of the grief and heartache of the parish ministry and of the ways in which that is compounded in a large church. They have had more sympathy for me as a person and more respect for me as a fellow journeyman preacher with them, practicing the craft of ministry at a level of competence they can respect, than have ministers in smaller situations who might be more inclined to pass off any success I may have had as merely that of being in that right place at the right time. They respect competence. They respect authenticity. They respect spiritual gifts. They respect sheer survival in the ministry in these days of such intense pressure for ministers. So the downtown, big-church-minister types have accorded me a kind of collegial comradeship, knowing full well that I have had a spiritual experience generally thought in mainline church circles to suggest instability and lack of credibility.

What Did the Conference and Larger Church Think?

The preceding section, while reporting on the reaction of ministerial colleagues, suggests also the mixed but generally positive reaction of "the larger church."

Ministers reading this would need to know that The Colonial Church of Edina, though approximately three thousand adult members, is not strictly a denominational church. We are a Congregational church that stayed out of the merger of the Congregational Christian Churches with the Evangelical and Reformed Church to create the now over twenty-five-year-old United Church of Christ. We have kept informal personal ties with both the UCC Congregationalists and the continuing National Association Congregationalists.

This means that Colonial's stance with the conference, or other instrumentalities of the whole fellowship of Congregationalists, has appeared to be equivocal. Colonial was one of the Congregational denomination's two "highest potential" churches in the postwar church building boom of the late 1940s and early 1950s.

Many denominational officials felt Colonial Church

could not prosper on its own. Instead it has grown from fifteen hundred in 1962 to over three thousand in 1981. Its budget has grown to just over $1 million for its regular ministries and missions in 1981. It has, at least in those terms, prospered.

The hardest fact for some denominational people to accept has been that this mainline church, in a very affluent suburb, grew with a distinctly evangelical theology, combined with a social concern and action stance, as well as a solid biblical and theological teaching stance. It spoke out against the imminent distortions in the presidency of Richard Nixon before Watergate when none of the major UCC churches of Minnesota, according to one of its own executives, was saying anything.

Colonial was controversial on a number of counts. It defied all the preconceptions about church leadership in the most generally affluent and powerful suburb of Minnesota. There it was, growing and extending itself in Edina even while it was offending many of its own economic and social power people and losing their membership and support. It was flourishing in a town full of well-off, well-educated, all-alike Scandinavian stock while drawing obvious street people into its Sunday congregations and into its membership. In a town full of the business community's leaders, Colonial was making it on the strength of the "little people"—the lower managers, the up-and-coming young people, the not-arrived.

The church refused to fold, despite its lack of denominational tie. Its mission grew and its contributions reached proportions larger than the mission budgets of some whole state conferences.

There was not much in our situation to make the church or me popular with the larger church. Yet the period of the ten years after my Spirit experience has been the very time, increasingly, when denominational people have been more and more willing to acknowledge that something was working at Colonial.

The UCC Minnesota State Conference executive early on became my friend. In my time of agonizing over whether to leave Colonial for the New York church, he several times phoned me at night to ask how I was. He asked, and he really wanted to know. He was my friend. His associate took much the same position.

My private feeling is that they were broad enough in spirit to care about the gospel ministry more than about denominational attachment, broad enough to be glad that a legitimate witness of Jesus was being made, even if it was not a ministry flying strictly under their colors.

I believe they were very much aware that their own denomination, nationally and in Minnesota, was shrinking in numbers while Colonial was growing. I believe they suspected Colonial was on to something theologically and spiritually, and so could find it in their hearts to wish us well.

Without a doubt they hoped Colonial might still join the national denomination. As an act of good faith Colonial did make a gift of $50,000 to the UCC Black College Fund. The United Church Board for Homeland Ministries made a large loan to Colonial to help with our new building project. I believe the personal respect from those executives was real and comradely in the best Christian sense.

Again, the ministers of the national UCC Consultation on the Large Church welcomed me on the basis of who I was and what I was doing in the ministry. They saw the materials from the church (as all churches were asked to share them). They came to have a sense that the Spirit of God was doing something at Colonial. They welcomed

me, invited me one year to tell them "the Colonial story."
Two years later they invited me to be one of their three
morning preachers—the first year they used their own
ministers as preachers to the group.

In public discussion they sincerely asked to hear the
story of my spiritual pilgrimage. I believe the telling won
me some friends. While it surely turned some off, it intrigued others. It's been an opportunity for a friendship
ministry to these brothers.

So, instead of punishment, the cutting off of friends, or
any kind of ostracizing, there has been a growing and
positive acceptance—even an emerging willingness to hear
something from the Colonial experience.

What Really Happened Inside That Large Congregation?

The congregation did not blow apart. No professional
staff left. One volunteer staff person seriously thought I
had lost my mind in the charismatic expressions of praise,
and the openness to healing and the practiced other gifts
of the Spirit. But generally the staff stayed, and most of
the members stayed.

There was much they did not understand. But generally, they were willing to learn.

I tried my best to teach them. I worked hard to learn
and understand the biblical base for the whole experience I
had had, and that I was commending to the church. I
made every effort to be open and above board. I took risks
some people thought were foolish. I shared my "tongue"
in public worship on Pentecost Sunday and on some other
occasions. Our most sophisticated staff member, our
newest teaching minister, gave active support to that. He
recognized that the Spirit is part of the gospel; Pentecost

[77]

cannot be expunged from the scriptural record nor denied its claim upon the church.

The Spirit experience fit with our Pilgrim, Puritan, Congregational, high Holy Spirit theological heritage. We tied the present day experience in with our long historical roots. We showed the Spirit experience to be integral to the life of the Congregational churches in colonial America. The Spirit had a solid anchor with us.

We did not go down in flames. The love of Jesus had already made itself manifest in our life. That fact prepared the people and me to receive the Holy Spirit. One by one and dozen by dozen they began to be baptized in the Spirit.

Enough other credible and creditable things were happening in Colonial's life to make the Spirit experience bearable. Indeed, love was at the heart of it—the very mark of the presence of God. Love rescued us.

Those who turned away in fear and anger have in some cases returned. The church has even achieved a place of leadership in the community that has encouraged some dubious members to hang on until they too understood and could be fully part of it.

The church's ministry on a wide front continued. We still have a superb youth program. We still do Bible teaching to the whole community. We still reach out in counseling to the troubled. We still call faithfully on the folks sick in hospital; still marry and bury and preach the Word Sunday by Sunday. Colonial Church and its life and experience was a lot for people to give up. Enough people gave me a chance and the church a chance so that we survived—together.

The only way churches ever survive is together. More than that, the experience was only part of what we were going through. A major building decision with accompanying land-buying and fund-raising certainly deflected some concern from our own home-grown Holy Spirit movement.

It is always important, I think, for a minister to be pastor to the people, loving them and shepherding them—especially through the times of church politics and issue differences. That means something to them: "that you still came to me in my need." They don't forget that. And it is probably that, that causes them to give their minister a chance, and to grant him or her the benefit of the doubt.

When that happens, it is God's own miracle. And that is the best answer as to what happened to The Colonial Church of Edina when the Spirit came into our safe church life.

Chapter 5

Questions About Receiving the Spirit

THE final and hardest question in the churches, the question that can so easily divide Christians and create controversy, is, I think, "Do I need to receive the Holy Spirit in order to be a Christian or to have a full Christian life?" How that question is answered, and the spirit with which it is answered, is critical.

If the baptism with the Holy Spirit becomes in any way a means for putting down one's fellow Christians, or of even faintly suggesting that all Christians who have not had this experience are second class, or worse, that those not baptized with the Spirit are not Christians at all, then only hurt and controversy and defensiveness and browbeating can come, along with all the division and self-righteousness with which most of us are already too familiar.

I do not believe any of that needs to occur. The potential problem is certainly there. It was there in the first-century church, as Paul's first letter to the Corinthians makes clear. But denominations, and congregations, and families do not need to be divided over who has the Spirit, and what's wrong with those who don't.

Who Has the Spirit?

In a sense, every Christian who has committed his or her life to Christ "has the Spirit." The only way any of us

[80]

know "God the Father and Christ the Son" in any personal way is through the Holy Spirit's bringing them to us. That is the role of the Spirit—bringing God close and making God real. The Spirit is the messenger, the ambassador, the translator, the conductor, the power line, the channel, the avenue for all of us to know God. Only the disciples of Jesus lived in a day when they knew Jesus the man personally—as well as God "the Father and Creator"—and then after Jesus' ascension, they knew the Holy Spirit as well. Pentecost birthed the church because the Spirit, in all the ages since the time of Jesus, brought the things of God to men and women.

I have already said that I felt the Spirit through my early life, and that I was a kind of Spirit person. But then came this new experience of the Spirit that was a baptism, a washing, a filling, a freshening. That experience didn't deny my earlier knowledge of the Spirit. It just meant the coming of the Spirit to me in a new way.

It seems very important to me that we of the Christian community allow our brothers and sisters to have many and different personal religious experiences without feeling that we all must have the same ones or have them in just the same way. Many of my parishioners have had experiences of faith that I have not had. Some have seen visions. Some have been "slain in the Spirit." Some have heard God speak to them—with audible sounds. Some have heard the Christmas angels sing. Some have seen Jesus—with their own eyes.

Must I envy them? Must I disparage their experience because I have not had it myself? Must I feel they're putting me down if they tell me with joy and excitement about the wonderful spiritual experience they've had? Of course not. Not if I have some shred of Christian maturity. Not if I pray daily for their growth in faith and experience.

Not if I believe in the "diversity of gifts" and experiences that Paul idealized.

To all this I say, "Terrific! Sounds wonderful! Praise God!"

Now, I do feel that the baptism with the Holy Spirit is more basic to the Christian life than most of these other experiences. I do believe that all Christians can be baptized with the Holy Spirit and, indeed, need to be if they and the church through them are to come into full power.

But the specific gifts they will receive in their baptizing will all be different. And the actual experience of baptism in the Spirit will be different for them than it was for me. It will also come at a different time in their lives, and on a different schedule, determined by their need, and by their own personal pilgrimage, their own *kairos,* their own "fullness of time."

I think I can afford to have patience about my people—as indeed they have had with me in so many ways—even though I would love them all to be baptized in the Holy Spirit right now. After all, I was forty-three before I received the baptism, and I know very well that I was not ready for it before that time; indeed, I had been a poor candidate for it, and probably could not have received it earlier because of particular problems in my own life. But aren't we all that way?

Until quite recently my wife had not received the baptism of the Spirit. Yet she loved me and valued highly what my baptism experience had meant to me and my life and ministry. She had again and again encouraged me to pursue the Spirit, to keep practicing my tongue of praise. Someday her own pilgrimage, I believed, would lead her into seeking and receiving that baptism. In the meantime, we were Christian comrades, brother and sister in faith together. And nothing prompted either of us to put the other down. I did not look on her as an unfulfilled Christian, nor did she see me as a browbeating, arrogant evangelist out to save her. She is saved. Christ saved her when she accepted and welcomed him into her heart.

At least two of our older children have received the baptism. It has helped them become deeply committed and mature Christians. In the past year our youngest son, at fifteen, came into a profound experience of the Spirit all on his own in the course of his own searching, his confirmation-year studying, his "heavy" conversations with his oldest sister about destiny and "the call" of God, and his listening one night to the music of the rock opera Godspell.

The Spirit, if you will, "fell upon him," and he spoke in tongues. On Pentecost Sunday, as many others came forward after church for prayers for the coming of the Spirit in their lives, he, too, came forward, the last one, and we wept and prayed in each other's arms, and praised God in tongues together, each in his own language of praise. At one particularly exalted moment of communion and love, while traveling across the country together on our way east for vacation time, he and I burst out together into spontaneous praise in tongues. A year later, his mother came forward for the baptism in the Pentecost service.

Is he a more mature Christian than his sisters, who have not had the experience? Not at all. He simply has his own unique, wonderful experience of the Spirit, which is his joy and strength.

Do I wish the baptism for all my family and all my flock? Of course. I want all Christians to have everything God has to offer them. I particularly want and pray for the church in America and in the world today to be baptized in the Spirit because this is God's offering of power to the church. Ultimately, that is the way and the means by which the church will be truly itself. Pentecost was a birth of power for the church so it could minister to the world. And the fear of the Spirit, the fear of spookiness, and emotionalism, and the Spirit's control of our lives rather than our own control, keeps Christians and churches from reaching their fullest potential.

Any Christian who loves Jesus is doing good. But I have no doubt that he or she could be braver, more daring, more willing to be a fool for Christ's sake, if the baptism with the Spirit was his or her experience with the wonderfully confirming sign of the particular (and least important but most universally available) gift of tongues. Because then there would be other gifts to work with—powers not of that Christian's own native ability, or training, or development, or cultivation.

In a day, such as our own time, of stark warfare against the forces of darkness, these gifts are desperately needed in every church. They need to be there in some people. They don't need to be there in all people. There is plenty of room for the pilgrimage and growth of the many sincere and seeking, and mature and wonderfully serving Christians who have not yet had, and may never have, that experience.

As "black and white together" is important for the church and the world, so is "pilgrims together"—Christians of varying and different experience, Christians at very different stages on their life pilgrimage.

I intend to keep offering my own congregation the opportunity to receive the Spirit—certainly each Pentecost Sunday, and at teaching sessions on the Spirit, and at other appropriate and appointed times.

After all, the presence of the Spirit in a person's life

through the new birth, the second baptism, which Jesus offered to Nicodemus, does make a difference.

Paul's great question in Acts 19, when he was traveling through Turkey to Ephesus and asked a group of disciples he found there, "Did you receive the Holy Spirit when you believed?" (or "Have you received the Holy Spirit since you believed?") indicates there was evidence of an incompleteness in them, something yet to be added.

Like many modern Christians, they confessed ignorance of the Spirit. It had not been part of their theology, as it has so often not been part of ours.

"By what baptism were you baptized?" asked Paul. "By John's." In other words, by the baptism of repentance. John had already said that the uniqueness of Jesus would be his baptism with the Spirit and power.

The baptism of repentance, of conversion, of changing your life, and receiving Christ, is *the first step,* the beginning, in the Christian life.

Isn't it logical that, as is true with everything else, as we grow, more should come?

Those disciples needed the full baptism of Jesus, Paul said, and so they were baptized by Paul, and when he laid his hands on them, "the Holy Spirit came upon them and they spoke in tongues of ecstasy and prophesied [Acts 19: 6, *NEB].*" They first were baptized with water—step number one in the Christian life. Then Paul laid hands on them and they were baptized with the Spirit—step number two in the Christian life.

Growth in Christian maturity, the individual pilgrimage of us all, is what receiving the Spirit is about, I think. Don't we all want to grow individually? Doesn't every parish church want to grow in depth and in numbers, reaching out and drawing all people to Christ?

If new life, rebirth, a second touch, is the unquestioned demand of the world itself upon the church and the churches today, then receiving the Holy Spirit, as the church did at Pentecost, can be the great expectation the church has as it heads toward the twenty-first century, and can be the greatest hope the world has as it goes into that century with us.